Be In
It to
WIN

Open More Doors. Close More Sales.

Be In It to WIN

STRATEGIES TO DEVELOP THE POSITIVE ATTITUDE YOU NEED FOR SALES SUCCESS

Gerhard Gschwandtner

Founder and Publisher of *Selling Power*

McGRAW-HILL

New York   Chicago   San Francisco   Lisbon
London   Madrid   Mexico City   Milan   New Delhi
San Juan   Seoul   Singapore   Sydney   Toronto

1 2 3 4 5 6 7 8 9 0   DOC/DOC   0 9 8 7 6

ISBN 0-07-147400-5

McGraw-Hill books are available at special quantity discounts to use as premiums and sales promotions, or for use in corporate training programs. For more information, please write to the Director of Special Sales, Professional Publishing, McGraw-Hill, Two Penn Plaza, New York, NY 10121-2298. Or contact your local bookstore.

 This book is printed on recycled, acid-free paper containing a minimum of 50% recycled, de-inked fiber.

Library of Congress Cataloging-in-Publication Data

Gschwandtner, Gerhard.
  Be in it to win : strategies to develop the positive attitude you need for sales success / Gerhard Gschwandtner.
      p.   cm.
  Includes index.
  ISBN 0-07-147400-5 (alk. paper)
    1. Selling—Psychological aspects.   2. Success in business—Psychological aspects.   I. Title.
  HF5438.8.P75G785   2006
  658.8501'9—dc22

                                         2006007027

Contents

A Note to the Reader   vii

PART 1

Success Secrets of the Masters: Interviews with Leading Motivational Thinkers   1

Chapter 1: Learning from the Giants: Great Motivational Leaders Show How to Find the Inner Flame   3

Chapter 2: The Zig Is Up: Zig Ziglar Shares His Lessons for Positive Living   15

Chapter 3: New Ways to Win with Wayne Dyer   23

Chapter 4: Dr. Norman Vincent Peale's Positive Thinking   39

Chapter 5: Dr. Denis Waitley: The Seeds of Greatness   61

Chapter 6: Tom Hopkins on Mastering the Art of Motivation   79

PART 2

Reach for the Sky: Surefire Strategies to Keep You Motivated and on Track for Success   93

Chapter 7: Destined for Success: Motivational Experts and Top Sales Performers Weigh In on What It Takes to Send Your Achievement Levels Soaring   95

CHAPTER 8: Stop Waiting for Happiness: Four
Ways to Pursue It   113

CHAPTER 9: Like Yourself Better: Seven Steps
for Becoming Your Own Best Friend   117

CHAPTER 10: Inquire Within: When Indecision Stalls
Your Quest for Success, Look Inward for Answers   119

CHAPTER 11: Focus on the Positive: 10 Rules
for Success   125

CHAPTER 12: Let Motivation Work Miracles: Five
Motivational Principles That Will Get You over
the Rough Spots   127

CHAPTER 13: Seek Out Opportunities: Proven Tips
for Purpose-Driven Sales   131

CHAPTER 14: Develop a Positive Attitude: Four
Methods for Keeping the Right Mindset   141

CHAPTER 15: Sales Manager's Training Guide: 12 Steps
to Improve Your Team's Ability to Cultivate a Positive
Attitude That Will Result in Better Sales   149

PART 3

MOTIVATIONAL HEROES: 35 TRUE STORIES
OF CHALLENGE AND ACHIEVEMENT   153

CREDITS   189

INDEX   193

A Note to the Reader

If you've ever needed a lift, felt like you weren't up to the task, wondered what your purpose was, or had a general, nagging feeling of self-doubt, this is the book for you. Collected in these pages is the wisdom of some of the great motivational thinkers, writers, and speakers of the past eight decades.

Yes, here they are in one-on-one interviews, in their own words answering specific, personal questions about their own challenges, setbacks, and motivational paths to fulfillment. Dr. Norman Vincent Peale (truly the greatest inspiration ever to motivate millions of people worldwide), Dr. Wayne Dyer, who taught us all about our erroneous zones, Dr. Denis Waitley, the first to champion the idea that athletes (and anyone else) could go beyond the records previously set, and many, many others. You'll find such motivators as Tom Hopkins, Omar Periu, and Zig Ziglar explaining in detail, with step-by-step lessons, how to motivate yourself and others to ever-greater accomplishments.

But that's not all. This book also contains the true motivational life stories of some of the most successful people from all walks of life. How about Jim Carrey—did you know that Jim and his siblings attended school by day, and then worked as security guards, assembly-line workers, and janitors by night? Or that Lee Iacocca was fired in July 1978 from Ford Motor

Company, where he had been president of the company for eight years, had been a Ford employee for 32 years, and had never worked anywhere else?

You may not know the story of an African American woman named C.J. Walker, who started her own hair products company in 1905 with $1.50 and became America's first woman self-made millionaire. Or, more recently, the story of Supreme Court Justice Ruth Bader Ginsburg, who graduated first among the women in her class at Cornell University, then earned admission to Harvard Law School, edited the prestigious *Harvard Law Review,* and finished Columbia Law School tied for first in her class. After all that accomplishment, the doors of opportunity should have opened wide; for Ruth Bader Ginsburg, however, they slammed shut. Still, she persevered.

As you can tell from reading just these few examples, each story in this book could help you find the motivation to overcome whatever you're facing now and in the future. When asked if you can ever graduate from needing motivation, Zig Ziglar said that motivation is like bathing or eating. You need to do it regularly to survive. Take this book as your motivation prescription. Read any part of it daily and watch your can-do attitude climb and your negativity disappear. Motivation isn't all you need to succeed, but it sure can help.

As you read this book, remember something that helped me when I faced challenges and adversity. Problems are nothing but wake-up calls for creativity. So wake up. Get motivated. And be creative.

Good Reading!
Gerhard Gschwandtner, Founder and Publisher,
Selling Power magazine

Be In It to WIN

❧———————————❧

PART 1

SUCCESS SECRETS OF THE MASTERS

❧———————————❧

Interviews with Leading Motivational Thinkers

CHAPTER 1

LEARNING FROM THE GIANTS

Great Motivational Leaders Show
How to Find the Inner Flame

ON JUNE 17, 1966, Paul E. Galanti, an experienced U.S. Navy pilot, took off from the USS *Hancock* in his A-4 Skyhawk to fly his ninety-seventh combat mission over Vietnam. Galanti, who defines *motivation* as "doing whatever the hell you have to do to get the job done," was about to approach his target area as antiaircraft fire hit his only jet engine. "When the engine got hit, the plane caught fire . . . it was rolling and tumbling," he recalls, describing the catastrophic experience. "The last thing I remember seeing (before the electricity went out) was 3,000 feet going down on the dial." As the plane went out of control, the tail blew off and Galanti tried frantically to establish radio contact with the other aircraft.

Smoke came into the cockpit and his mind flashed the warning, "You're supposed to slow down the airplane as much as you can before ejecting." The controls failed to respond to the pilot's commands. Every split second counted as the plane approached the ground in a dizzying falling, tumbling, and rolling pattern. Galanti kept his cool. "There is a face curtain in the head rest of the seat. You simply pull it over your face to shield your face from the wind blast. That fires a rocket from under the seat, it blows off the canopy, and you're ejected out of the airplane." The powerful wind resistance stretched virtually every joint in his body, and Galanti felt excruciating pain.

The parachute opened safely. As he approached the ground, looking for a safe spot to land, he was shot in his neck. "The shot blew out the whole back of my helmet," he remembers. "I didn't even realize until I hit the ground that there was blood all over the flight suit." A group of North Vietnamese captured Galanti and put him up against a tree with their rifles pointing against him. "It was a very interesting sensation—standing there, with all these rifles pointing at me. These guys were mad." Galanti pauses and changes the subject. "Getting shot down ruins your entire day . . . [he grins] but on the bright side, I probably would have never made a parachute jump if it hadn't been for that lucky shot."

So, what went through his mind when these rifles were pointing at him? "I kept looking at all these little holes and thinking, I wonder if I'll ever see the bullet," says Galanti. "There wasn't anything I could do. But finally one guy started yelling and pushing them away and he grabbed me and took charge of me. I don't know who he was. Then a guy with a cross on his arm—a medic—came up and poured some iodine over my neck and shoulder."

"Did you have some way of dealing with this situation that allowed you to keep your cool?" I probe.

"I don't remember ever going into a cold panic. I was watching this experience as if it were happening to someone else. Like I was a bird up in the sky. I felt sorry for this guy, but it wasn't a big deal."

Paul Galanti used this visualization technique—"as if it were happening to someone else"—several times before. "I am a lot more objective that way when I am in a tight situation," he explains. "Every time something bad is going to happen, this little thing just watches and checks all around." Galanti spent almost seven years in a North Vietnamese prison camp until his release on February 12, 1973. His photograph appeared on the covers of *Newsweek* and *Life* magazines. He remained in the navy for another nine years, serving as the head of navy recruiting (a sales job, as he calls it) and as battalion officer responsible for leadership training. Paul Galanti's technique for coping with an extremely demotivating situation is known as the "as-if" technique. It consists of purposely stepping into a new role, thus releasing untapped energies made available through imagination. Imagination is a powerful source of motivation. Professional actors use their imaginations to act their way into a new role and a new feeling. All good acting starts with the mental as-if technique.

Galanti stepped out of his role as prisoner of war and became—for the time period he was in danger—that detached observer in the sky, watching the prisoner being lined up against a tree. This made his prisoner's experience "not a big deal" and thus tolerable. He kept his sanity in an inhuman situation and maintained a high level of motivation throughout his ordeal as a POW. He never lost a night's sleep over his experience back in the United States, and he's one of the happiest people I've ever met. The as-if technique is not only used as a survival tool or as a method for professional actors, but also as an effective strategy for dealing with potentially demotivating situations in selling.

Mary Kay Ash, founder of Mary Kay cosmetics, recommends, "Act enthusiastic—even when you don't feel like it. I've found that acting enthusiastically causes you to become enthusiastic. If someone asks how are you, the answer is *great*— even if you aren't." Someone once said, "Fake it 'til you make it." She certainly made it. Tom Hopkins, one of America's leading sales trainers, gives similar advice. "There's an old saying, 'the show must go on,' and there are days when I'm tired and I go out there on stage and do what I am dedicated to doing. You have no choice—you have to give it the best you've got. What happens is that when you're giving your best, all of a sudden your adrenaline kicks in and you're doing great.

"If you're talking to a customer and if you're not feeling good, you literally start acting as if you were happy to talk to your prospect. All of a sudden you start listening and saying to yourself, 'Hey, I am going to close a large transaction here!' " Interestingly, Tom Hopkins and Mary Kay define *motivation* as an ability. Hopkins sees it as "the ability to get people to stretch further than they are accustomed to in order to reach their goals."

Mary Kay says, "Motivation is the ability to inspire a person—to reach down within himself or herself, to bring to fruition those wonderful 'seeds of greatness' that God planted in each of us. It's said that the average person uses only about 10 percent of his God-given ability. Most of us die with our music still unplayed. Motivation encourages people to do what they've always dreamed of doing."

THE IMPORTANCE OF MENTORS AND HEROES

Zig Ziglar, America's number one motivator, once compared motivation to the role of a starter in a car that cranks up the engine. Without the starter, the engine would never utilize the available horsepower. When Zig was in high school, he hated history. Zig explains, "I hated the thought of having to learn something that happened 200 years ago. So my history teacher spent some time selling me on why I had to know my history. He said that if I had any ability that extended beyond earning a living, I had a moral responsibility, an obligation to take that ability and make a contribution to my fellow man and my country." Zig pointed to his teacher's compelling logic, "You're part of society, and if everybody doesn't make a contribution toward making it better—regardless of how much ability you might have or how individually successful you might be—if your society has major flaws, then your individual contribution has less value."

Zig Ziglar's mentor, Joe Harris, may well have started the powerful engine that led the Ziglar Corporation to a level of success far beyond the dreams of its founder. A little-known fact among the many people who have known Zig for years is that his corporate mission statement begins, "The purpose of the Zig Ziglar Corporation is to help people more fully utilize their physical, mental, and spiritual abilities in order to contribute to the betterment of society . . ." It is not uncommon that even a hero's negative comments can, like a photonegative, produce positive results. Tom Hopkins recollects, "My father wanted me to become a famous attorney, and I only lasted about 90 days in college. I came home and told my father that I quit and he was very disappointed. He said, 'I will always love you, even though you'll never amount to any-thing.' This really was a tremendous emotional and psycho-logical motivator, because I literally told myself, 'Okay, I'm going to prove that I can become a success.' " Tom's father started the engine. Tom hurt at the moment, but he healed over a lifetime.

Dr. Denis Waitley, the author of the best-selling audiocas-sette program *The Psychology of Winning* (Nightingale-Conant Corp., Chicago) was significantly influenced by his father at a much earlier age. "He came into my room and sat down on my bed and gave me the belief that I was special, that I had a destiny, that I had a great purpose. He blew out the light and at the same time he would lean against the switch. I thought it was magic. He told me, 'Notice how it gets dark when your light is out. It is out everywhere. The only world you'll ever know is the one you see with your eyes.' He said that life is in the perception of the eyes of the beholder. 'When you are asleep, the world is asleep. When you arise in the morning, the whole world wakes up, when you feel sick, the whole world is a sick place, and when you're happy, the world is beautiful. Therefore, in your journey of life, you'll notice people being different. But the thing is that they are only seeing it from their eyes—and it's unique.' " What did Dr. Waitley learn from his hero? "You can change the outcome of the world simply by the way you view it, and that's the important thing to know." After a reflective pause he adds, "That still is the greatest thing I've ever learned. That's what perception is all about." Mentors and heroes can help us chart our course in life, yet we alone are responsible for the trip. But how do we cope with the demotivators—the currents of fear and worry in the stream of life?

DEALING WITH DEMOTIVATORS

"The single most unrewarded of all human emotions is worry," explains Steven McMillan, a chairman and CEO of Electrolux, a company with a sales force of 28,000 people. "It doesn't accomplish anything. There is no positive result from worry, yet all of us do it from time to time. I see it every day in our business. We tend to explode problems way beyond what they really represent. I hear people saying, 'Steve, this is really a big problem,' and they're totally overwhelmed. "The reason problems really become overwhelming is because we don't have a methodology to sit down and think it through. Worrying about it won't help you. But if you say, 'I have identified a problem of an obstacle we have to get over,' then we can say, 'Fine, we've identified that obstacle, now let's get down and look at it from an analytical point of view. Let's think about what our options are. If the obstacle is too high, let's get around it. If it's too wide, then let's go over it. If we can't go over or around it, then let's go under it.' In all too many cases, we react quickly and superficially without thinking it through. Therefore, we worry. It's a terrible waste of time."

McMillan, a graduate of Harvard Business School—a school famous for its case study method—has added a new dimension to the word *motivation*. "I define motivation as a combination of four elements. One is the opportunity. You can't motivate someone without having a real opportunity. The business objective has to be real. The second element is education—the how-to skills. Motivation without education equals frustration. The third part is hype. It's fun, it's enjoyable, but hype by itself is not going to generate positive, long-term action. The last element is an analytical methodology for dealing with problems. "Motivation is more than just having the will to solve a problem," he continues. "It's also having the methodology with which to approach a problem. To me, these elements together lead to a genuine motivation and worthwhile action."

Dr. Norman Vincent Peale, who until his death was America's number one authority on positive thinking, told us about the preventive steps of dealing with demotivating experiences. "You know, a salesperson out on the road is alone. This feeling can siphon off his motivation. I think that the best method is to go to your room and read a good motivational book. Carry such literature around. Saturate your mind with motivational material. The evening news is likely to be depressing and negative. If you fill your mind with positive thoughts, they soak into your subconscious, so that when you get up the next day, you are going to have a great day." Dr. Peale also urges salespeople to use positive affirmations. "To me, the most powerful form of self-direction is that of affirmation. If I say, 'Oh, I wish I felt better today!' that's not an affirmation. That's a depreciation. But if you say, 'I feel good today and I thank God for it and I'm going to have a great day!' then your subconscious mind will listen to that strong declaration. I've done this 10,000 times and I couldn't get along without it."

To Dr. Peale, the process of motivation begins with self-commitment. The powerful expectation to have a great day will lead to a great day. And if problems arise? Dr. Peale quips, "The only people that I ever have known to have no problems are in the cemetery." His advice is to attack problems squarely because, "Every problem contains the seed to its own solution." There is a certain comfort to knowing that, when we think that we have reached the end of our road, we really have only reached the end of our creativity. Talking to Dr. Peale on several occasions convinced me that problems are nothing but wake-up calls for creativity.

OVERCOMING DISAPPOINTMENT

"A few years ago, I saw a slogan in a car dealership," says Bob Baseman, executive vice president of sales for Encyclopedia Britannica (USA). "It was six feet wide and three feet high. The sign asked, 'Mr. and Mrs. Prospect, just what was it that you were so worried about one year ago today?' " Baseman, who leads over 3,000 salespeople, expands, "I think this is applicable to life. "I woke up one morning when I was 25 years old and I discovered that the world had ended because my father had died. It was a crushing blow. I looked through the window and I saw a man going to work and I saw children going to school and I wanted to scream at the top of my lungs, 'Hey, don't you know the world is over!' But you know what? It wasn't over. Unfortunately, it was a very, very difficult lesson to learn all at one time. But I don't think you can accomplish anything worrying about that which you can't control." Baseman has grown from the disappointment and he has become the number one attitude builder in his company. According to him, *attitude* is the most overlooked secret in the face of disappointment.

Ed Foreman, the son of a New Mexico dirt farmer, is the only person in the twentieth century to have been elected to the U.S. Congress from two different states: Texas in 1962 and New Mexico in 1968. Ed described his most disappointing experience as follows.

"I've had a lot of them. I guess it was losing the reelection to Congress. I had done a beautiful job, but 51 percent of the people decided they wanted someone else to represent them. I had been working my heart out for what I believed was best for them and my country. I went around for about a month feeling like someone hit me in the gut with his fist and knocked all the air out of me. At night I would dream that the election had not yet been held and that I was going to win."

One day when Ed felt particularly gloomy, his five-year-old daughter walked up to him saying, "Daddy, the next time you run for office, why don't you run in an area where there are more Republicans than Democrats?"

Foreman's prescription for self-motivation after disappointment: "You must immediately occupy yourself with something that can get you excited. I started another business. I got excited about that and flat forgot about the political defeat. It became a minor learning experience." To Foreman, motivation is "excitement about and for life and for what you do." The excitement of a new challenge has brought new meaning to his life.

Rich DeVos, cofounder of Amway, put his fight with the Canadian government at the top of his list of demotivating experiences. "Just to be accused of wrongdoing—but you know within you that you've done everything that was right— and then to have to admit to being wrong, even though you followed expert advice, was a very demotivating thing. But finally, you have to stand up; if you're the head of the company, then you have to be responsible for the action of everybody. As time goes by, you kind of get over that."

DeVos feels that developing coping strategies for dealing with disappointment is part of leadership. "You've got to be able to think while the bullets are flying. You've got to stay cool in business and keep going. I think that's a sense of knowing who you are. If you are comfortable with who you are and know you're not perfect and accept the fact that you don't have all the answers . . . you just work with what you've got and then you move forward." DeVos and his partner built a billion-dollar business with over a million salespeople worldwide.

Here is another piece of evidence that leads to the paradoxical question, "Isn't disappointment at the root of every growth experience?" The disappointing event leads to self-discovery, and we learn another lesson of who we really are. The Socratic advice "know thyself" could be changed to "know thy motivation," for if you really discover what moves you, you'll know your direction and move forward with confidence.

As many of these compelling life stories of successful leaders, motivators, and business executives suggest, resolved disappointment is the cradle of motivation and ultimately responsible for our ambitions and success in life. Unresolved disappointment leads to cynicism, the greatest destroyer of motivation.

Dr. Wayne Dyer, the author of several international bestsellers (*The Sky's the Limit, Pulling Your Own Strings,* and *Gifts from Eykis*), pointed to this fact when we talked about the requirements for an atmosphere or climate in which people can be motivated, "People who have a sourpuss attitude toward life are likely to get serious diseases." And what are the characteristics of a motivating attitude that creates a climate of motivation? "It's a state of acceptance of where the other person is," explains Dr. Dyer, "rather than where you would like him or her to be. Carl Rogers called it 'unconditional, positive regard!' It means being nonjudgmental. It means being able to provide a fun environment where life is not taken so seriously. If you look at all your most favorite people in life, the one characteristic that runs through them all is that they know how to laugh. It's what I call an unhostile sense of humor."

The cynical person's sense of humor is full of hostility while the accepting person's humor is disarming. Dr. Dyer pokes fun at himself in his lectures across the country, "I always talk about my baldness and the dumb things I've done in my life. When people see that you're not hostile, they open up." Dr. Dyer sees his role as motivator as being a tour guide to our inner potential. "A good motivator helps you discover your own potential." In Dr. Dyer's book *What Do You Really Want for Your Children?* he postulates that the only real motivation is inner motivation. "I teach my children that they have an inner candle flame that must never flicker. The outer candle flame can be blown out at any time, but if you love yourself and if you are positive in that, then no matter who comes along to try to convince you otherwise, that inner flame will never flicker."

CHAPTER 2

THE ZIG IS UP

❧⎯⎯⎯⎯⎯❧

Zig Ziglar Shares His Lessons for Positive Living

ZIG ZIGLAR HAS HELPED millions find the ability and drive to succeed. For more than 30 years this motivational marvel has wowed audiences around the world with his simple yet penetrating insight into personal achievement. His books have been translated into 32 languages, and his name recognition among Americans hovers at an astounding 36 percent.

Ziglar's message transcends mere motivational speaking. While he believes that attitude plays a key role in determining success, Ziglar stresses the importance of balancing a positive attitude with the hands-on abilities necessary to accomplish our dreams. As always, Ziglar has a ready anecdote to illustrate his point.

"When I was in the seventh grade I went out for the boxing team. I weighed a whopping 82 pounds. I was very confident because I had enjoyed a certain amount of success as a playground gladiator. The guy I was going to spar with weighed about 62 pounds and I just knew I'd kill him. What I did not realize was that he had been on the team for two years already. It took him about three seconds to figure out that the straightest distance to my nose was a left jab. Two seconds later he figured it out again. And again and again. Since more than my feelings were getting hurt I decided I was too busy for the boxing team.

"But then the coach took me aside and started teaching me some fundamentals. Within a couple of weeks I was able to hit my opponent once in a while. I quickly learned that the hitter had more fun than the hittee. After about three or four weeks I was actually winning. And the point here is that when I went into the ring the first time, I had a great attitude; I was positive, optimistic, enthusiastic, and highly motivated; but I was about to get killed. When I added the skill to the attitude my effectiveness went way up. Neither attitude nor ability alone will get you there—you need them both to be successful."

Besides attitude and ability, Ziglar's recipe for success includes many additional ingredients. Part of the problem facing many people, he says, is that they lack a clear destination in life. And without a destination in mind it's nearly impossible to find your way. By contrast, Ziglar can enunciate a clear definition of success.

"Many people are mistaken in equating success solely with money," he says. "To me, success means getting a reasonable amount of the things money will buy and all of the things money won't buy. Money is not the most important thing, but when you need it there are few substitutes. While I like the things money can buy, I love what money won't buy. It bought me a house, but it won't buy me a home. It would buy me a companion, but it won't buy me a friend.

"Then the second part of what success means relates to when you've dealt with the physical, mental, and spiritual aspects of life. If I made millions and destroyed my health in the process, or neglected my family, that's not success."

Unlike some speakers who talk a good game but fail to live up to the ideals they espouse, credibility is not an issue for Zig Ziglar. If he talks the talk, he walks the walk, too. When he tells an audience that physical fitness will increase their energy, help them perform better, and improve their lives, he's speaking from experience.

"Twenty-five years ago I made a decision to do something about physical fitness," he says. "Since then I've been eating sensibly and exercising regularly. Today my exercise regimen includes vigorous walking five to seven times a week, a 20-minute routine involving push-ups, and stretching as well as weightlifting. Now at age 70, I can stay on the treadmill five minutes longer than I could when I was 45. That means that I have more documented energy today than I did 25 years ago. Does that enable me to be more productive? Of course it does. Do I have more fun at it? Absolutely.

"Now some people say, 'I have been smoking and drinking for 35 years and it has never hurt me.' But what they don't know is how great they could have been had they abstained from those things from the start. Right now I'm more enthusiastic than ever about exercise and diet because I have so many plans. And to be able to reach my other goals I have to reach my physical goals, too."

Anyone who has seen Zig Ziglar speak can attest to his enthusiasm and vigor. This bountiful energy helps Ziglar maintain a travel schedule that would daunt many a newcomer to the motivation field. Surprisingly, whether he has given the same talk 5 or 500 times, Ziglar always dedicates at least three hours to preparing for each show.

"The majority of that time I will simply be giving the talk mentally. But this is essential, because it frees up my creative side. My left brain is so totally trained on that area that it frees my right brain to be creative. And I guarantee you that there will be some creative thoughts, ideas, or a release of information as a result of combining these things that will make a difference. And that is the way creativity works."

Despite his phenomenal success, the result of hundreds of thousands of appreciative and satisfied customers, Ziglar still hears the familiar refrain that motivational speakers fail to produce long-term results. In a way, he says, he fully agrees. "A reporter once asked me how I responded to the charge that motivation is not permanent," Ziglar explains. "I said, 'Absolutely right!' It is not permanent. Neither is bathing. But if you bathe every day you're going to smell good. In my seminars I explain that 15 minutes a day of motivation from a good audiocassette or a book can make a tremendous difference in your life and give you a motivational lift every day.

"As a matter of fact, until just recently, one of the mysteries that had plagued me for a long time was why we get approximately 200 times as many testimonial letters from people who have read my books or listened to my tapes as from people who saw me appear in person. And while we get tremendous responses from the speeches, I discovered the reason for this discrepancy from a study done by Stanford University. They found that 95 percent of the people who believe in the concepts we talk about—who know they need to have goals, the right attitude, the applicable skills—they are unable to implement this philosophy because they don't have the resources to follow through. They don't have the tapes or the book to refer to and follow up with repetition. And that study's results reinforced what I have always believed: that repetition is the mother of learning and the father of action, which means it is the architect of accomplishment."

Recently, Ziglar and his family suffered their greatest personal adversity when his daughter, Suzy, died tragically after a protracted battle with pulmonary fibrosis. While he admits to enduring extraordinary turmoil over the tragedy, Ziglar says that he has emerged from the experience with a renewed faith and positive outlook on life, which he shares in his book, *Confessions of a Grieving Christian*.

"What I want to share in the book," Ziglar says, "is that there is a hope that goes beyond anything we can possibly expect. In fact, it's more of a journal in that I share my thoughts and feelings as I felt them, especially as they remind me of her. In Dallas recently we had some snow, and my other children and wife and I all started weeping because Suzy had a passion for snow. If she saw one snowflake she would tell everyone that she was going into her snow dance to produce six to eight inches of snow. So the snow brings back that memory. The book encourages people to let the tears flow and to give people credit for good intentions when they say they know how you feel. Because nothing compares to losing a child. In the natural order of things she was supposed to come to my funeral, not the other way around. So I encourage people, don't deny your grief, let the tears flow, but look to the source of all joy and know that God is really in control."

GOAL SETTING FROM THE MASTER

Everyone formulates goals. Yet surprisingly few people embrace a goals' program encompassing the areas of life that can yield sustainable dividends. Zig Ziglar can help you change all that. Follow his six-step lesson plan for developing a long-term goals' program and you'll be on your way.

1. *Balance your objectives.* Write out everything you want to be, do, or have. Sit on this list for a couple of days; then write next to each item in one sentence why you want to be, do, or have that. If you can't do it in one sentence it's not a realistic objective for now. Draw a line through it. This should reduce your list to a manageable number of items. That's important, because you can't have everything right now that you want.

2. *Evaluate your list.* Look at the list and ask yourself, "If I had, did, and tried all of these things, would I be happy, healthy, prosperous, secure, and have friends, strong family relationships, and peace of mind?" In other words, would your life be in balance? If you answer no, then you need to break down the list some more.

3. *Separate into threes.* Divide your list into short-range goals that can be accomplished in a month or less, intermediate goals that may take up to a year, and long-range goals in excess of a year. Now look over your list and make sure it is equally balanced among the three. Eliminate goals in the area that is overloaded.

4. *Ask five key questions.* For each item on your list, ask yourself: (1) "Is this really my goal?" Do you want that car because it's best for you, or because your neighbor

has one? These goals must be for your fulfillment, so that's an important question. (2) "Is it morally right and fair to everyone concerned?" If you want a new shotgun but your daughter needs braces, you may not be able to have them both. (3) "Will reaching this goal take me closer to or further away from my major objective in life?" That ski weekend may look enticing, but if you have the chance to break a sales record, then you should consider the long-term gratification that the award will bring as opposed to the short-term pleasure of a ski trip. (4) "Can I emotionally commit to reaching this goal?" We make decisions based on emotions. So you need to acknowledge that the emotional commitment is just as important as the intellectual commitment. (5) "With this plan of action, can I realistically see myself reaching this goal?" Can you visualize yourself there? It's very important that you believe in yourself enough to visualize it ahead of time. Asking these five questions should reduce your list even more so that you're ready for the next step.

5. *Run the goal test.* Write your goals down again, then look at each one and consider what the benefits are of reaching that goal. Next, ask yourself what obstacles stand in your way. With these obstacles in mind, what do you need to know to get there? Identify the people, groups, and organizations that you need to work with in order to get there. Then write down your specific action plan, from steps 1 to 100, if necessary, that will bring you to what you're trying to accomplish.

6. *Set a date.* A lot of people set dates without considering the demands of the situation. So you should set a realistic date for accomplishing this goal that takes into

account all the factors you have determined in step 5. Out of this process, Ziglar says, you should wind up with a balanced list including both your large-scale and less ambitious goals. "The big goals should be out of reach," Ziglar explains, "but not out of sight. That is critical, because the long-range goals help you over-come short-range frustration. Keeping one eye on the distant goal helps you move beyond these obstacles." Then some goals must be daily because that gives you a sense of accomplishment along the way. I recommend that at the end of every day you look back and write down what you accomplished that day and a comment about how it made a difference in making your dreams a reality. You will stave off negative thinking and denial and wind up with a daily chart that leads directly to a successful outcome.

CHAPTER 3

NEW WAYS TO WIN
WITH WAYNE DYER

D R. WAYNE DYER, SUPERSALESMAN, worldwide lecturer and TV personality, is the number one best-selling
author of such life changing books as *Your Erroneous Zones,*
Pulling Your Own Strings, and *The Sky's the Limit.* In the years
since *Your Erroneous Zones* was published, Dyer has spawned
dozens of imitators, yet he remains the acknowledged Father
of Motivation. Perhaps more than any other man of his generation, Dyer has managed to embody the spirit of the times, or
even lead it a little. His true genius may lie in his ability to
anticipate the mood of the people, so that he appears not
merely timely, but prescient. Time and again, the arrival of a
new Wayne Dyer book acts like a magnetic pole of the spirit,
tugging our storm-tossed lives onto a firm course. Dyer is at

the helm, pointing us in the right direction. Only a few years ago, he boldly introduced the concept of the "no-limit person" one can become. He proposed to cut through the tangle of negative emotions, habits, and obligations that bind us to the ground. Dr. Dyer offers an eye-opening message of hope, freedom, and challenge, as well as a clear picture of his inner blueprint to success.

Question: Do you consider yourself a good salesman?

Dr. Dyer: I do. I have been called one of the top salesmen in the publishing field. People say I am a terrific book salesman. However, I have never made a conscious effort to sell anything in my life, and yet, I know that I am an excellent salesman.

Question: What did you do to become an excellent salesman?

Dr. Dyer: I achieve inner serenity. I don't believe in pushing my products on anyone else. I think I am a good salesman because when I'm on the air, I just sell myself. I talk common sense. I talk from a perspective of being someone that other people would want to hear and know more about. And as a result—and that's even done unconsciously— people then want to go out and buy my books to know more about what I do.

Question: You say it's done unconsciously. What subconscious message to you communicate?

Dr. Dyer: You simply sell yourself. You believe in who you are and what you do. I believe in the concept of modeling. You have to model whatever it is you're asking somebody else to become.

Question: So, in selling, the first product you have to be concerned with is yourself?

Dr. Dyer: Right. In my book, *Gifts from Eykis,* I use a quote from Thoreau describing what I mean: "If one advances confidently in the direction of his own dreams, and endeavors to live the life which he has imagined, he will meet with a success unexpected in common hours." If you're a person who really, truly believes in yourself and the possibility of reaching your dreams, then that will come through and other people will want more of you. This also applies to the products you're associated with.

Question: You seem to describe charisma.

Dr. Dyer: Yes, I think of it as an enthusiasm for life. It is a genuine excitement of who you are and what you are doing. Translated into selling, it means that you communicate to other people that you really care about them as people, rather than as buyers of your product.

Question: Could you tell us about your first major sale and how you have applied this technique?

Dr. Dyer: I think my biggest sale was my book, *Your Erroneous Zones.* When I met with the publisher's editorial vice president to talk about the sale of my manuscript, I realized that he had just experienced a personal setback in his life. He was upset about it. I stayed in his office for four hours and we discussed the book all afternoon. We talked about a problem that we both had faced in our lives. I talked to him from a perspective of a caring person. I suspended all my desire to get my book published. I was just doing what seemed to make sense to me at that moment, trusting my inner instincts. The next day he called and told me they were going to publish my book.

Question: It appears that your ability to suspend your preoccupation with selling your book was the key to the sale.
Dr. Dyer: Yes, human love, the ability to reach out to a person, is the greatest sales technique in the world.

ONENESS . . . AND COOPERATIVE SELLING

Dyer's views on selling and business are a natural outgrowth of his philosophy of oneness. Simply put, he believes that all of us here on earth are part of a greater organism. Competition does not get much play in this worldview, he reasons, or it shouldn't. Using the analogy of the human body, Dyer feels that it's unhealthy, even impossible, for one part of the anatomy to oppose another. Every cell works in unison with its counterpart. The uncooperative cell is an anomaly, a cancer. In the absence of cancer, the cells are joined in a harmonious balance that benefits the whole. Dyer calls this harmony *oneness*. If we can bring this concept into our lives as salespeople, it's possible to see that competition is an illusion. You don't have to sell against somebody else when you are so supremely good at selling for yourself and your company to benefit the customer. You don't have to reach into your salesperson's bag of tricks to nab the sale at all costs when you truly believe that you're working for the customer, that your interests and the customer's are the same.

"In order to be good at selling, you have to fall in love with what you do, and then sell that love," says Dyer. You don't sell your product, because every product in the world has some validity, and there is another product out there that will satisfy the customer's need just as well.

"The most successful salespeople in the world are the ones who have the most serenity," he adds. "They're working for the customer's quota, not their own. Uppermost in their minds is the question, 'How can I serve you?' " Dyer sees the spirit at work in everything we do in sales, whether making the presentation, prospecting, or performing follow-up customer service. The difference between superachievers and average performers is enthusiasm, or what's called "the God within" by Dyer. "When you are filled with enthusiasm for what you sell, and can convey that, it doesn't matter what product you're offering—the people will want it."

Dyer's concept of oneness, applied to sales, is a logical extension of the ideas he developed over two decades. First work on yourself and your attitude. Then externalize it. Apply what you've learned along the path to self-fulfillment so that you can better serve your customers. Make cooperation and service the rule in all your business dealings.

Question: In your opinion, what are the key characteristics of an effective salesperson?

Dr. Dyer: I think first and foremost of someone who has positive self-values, self-worth, self-esteem. That is at the very top. When you don't have that, then all of the other things don't make any difference. In addition, you should have the ability to communicate a feeling of enthusiasm, a feeling of excitement about who you are and what you're selling, being a model, being flexible, and having a sense of humor.

Question: What are the keys to improving your relationship with a customer or prospect?

Dr. Dyer: It all boils down to what they need and what I can provide. It means shifting your concern from problems to solutions. Solution-oriented thinking comes from caring and loving. You have to see things through the eyes of the other person. You should be so involved in helping another human being that your own needs became unimportant.

Question: How about the problem customer? What do you feel are the most significant barriers?

Dr. Dyer: I honestly believe they are all within ourselves. To me, there are no barriers, only challenges.

Question: Have you ever counseled salespeople on an individual basis?

Dr. Dyer: I've done a lot of that.

Question: What do you feel are the most common obstacles that salespeople seem to put in their own way?

Dr. Dyer: The biggest one is the fear of failure. Equating their performance on the job with who they are as a person.

Question: What do you mean by that?

Dr. Dyer: In other words, they are telling themselves, "If I make the sale, I can be happy. If I don't make the sale, I can't be happy." Consequently, with economic conditions bad, interest rates high, money hard to get, they are bound to be depressed.

Question: Do you ever experience the fear of failure when you write a book or appear on national television?

Dr. Dyer: No. I learned something very important. When I write, I write for myself. When I first starting writing, I submitted 100 articles that were rejected. Anybody in his right mind would have said, "Okay, I'm not a writer; they are rejecting my articles." It never made a bit of difference to me. I didn't judge myself as a failure based on what other people think I should have done. It was just one more opportunity to learn and to prove that I could do something. When I give a speech, I must first please myself. I believe in what I do and I get my satisfaction from completing it.

Question: So, you don't care about whether people will buy?

Dr. Dyer: It's the work itself; it's what I do that counts. If they buy, it's just a bonus. It's advancing confidently in the direction of your own dream. . . .

Question: Do you care about the positive reactions?

Dr. Dyer: I love to hear positive reactions from people. I like getting good book sales. These are all wonderful things. I want them, but I don't need them. Ironically, you will meet with success in selling if you don't need to make the sale. That's the key. So, if I don't sell one book, I'm okay.

Question: That's a tough act to follow. If a salesperson doesn't make that big sale, he or she isn't likely to say, "I'm okay."

Dr. Dyer: It's your choice. You don't need to interpret a lost sale as a rejection of yourself. If you need the sale to prove your self-worth, you will end up trying too hard. You'll be communicating that if you don't get it, you're going to be hurt, you're going to feel bad. So you'll come across as pushy; you'll be tempted to use guilt. All this comes from needing the sale. But you've got the choice to turn this around by conveying to that person, "If I make the sale, that's terrific; if I don't make the sale, that's fine, too. I like you and maybe we'll do business some other time."

Question: It sounds as if you don't believe that striving for the number one spot in your field is a good idea.

Dr. Dyer: I think that is a very unhealthy, sick kind of concept.

Question: One of the most successful films in the field of sales motivation, titled *Second Effort,* has sold nearly 10,000 copies in the past 10 years. The basic message is Vince Lombardi's famous quote, "Winning is the only thing."

Dr. Dyer: I disagree vehemently.

Question: Why?

Dr. Dyer: First of all, you cannot win all the time. Lombardi knew that. He was a great motivator, not because of his emphasis on winning, but because he knew how to appeal to each one of his players on an individual, personal basis. Lombardi himself did not win all the time. He had to drink milk the last 10 years of his life because of his ulcers; he was grossly overweight and died a very premature death. If you have to tell yourself that winning is the only thing, or if you define winning as having to beat somebody, you're going to be a loser. You can't win all the time. Even Muhammad Ali, who was "the greatest," lost sometimes!

Question: So, in selling, you could win more sales not by concentrating on winning but by . . .

Dr. Dyer: When you depend on competition to win, you are putting somebody else in charge of your life. If you give up control over your emotional life, you're bound to suffer. When you're looking over your shoulder at the other guy

PERSONAL TRANSFORMATION

Dyer believes that personal transformation results from the simple act of being willing to recognize our higher selves. "Be willing and forget determination," he says. You can't will yourself to succeed any more than you can force a plant to grow. But if you water the plant, provide it with the proper nutrients and sunlight, it will grow all on its own. Trying to change in order to achieve success is as pointless as tugging on the shoots of the plant. To those among us schooled in the American Way of hard work and competition, this may be a little hard to swallow. From the earliest age we're taught to sweat for what we get. The idea that success will just come to us if we let it seems almost heretical. Looking at this side of Dyer in light of his grounding in Asian philosophy makes the concept a little easier to grasp. His views on willingness or openness to change are akin to the Zen notion of *satori,* or instant enlightenment. Many Buddhists believe that self-actualization results not from years of study and meditation (i.e., from striving), but from the lightning-quick realization that we are already perfectly functioning, fulfilled beings, that each of us already has all we need to be happy and whole. This sudden awakening of the self to its innate riches is what Dyer is talking about. But where does one begin? "By recognizing that who you are is not your form, that you are more than the body you occupy," Dyer says. "Recognize that what makes you human is not this form, but the invisible intelligence that suffuses you—mind, spirit, God, whatever you want to call it."

and then deciding whether or not you are doing well based on comparing yourself with him, then he's in charge of your life. By looking over your shoulder, you'll end up losing; by looking inside, you'll find the key to growth, self-improvement, and happiness.

Question: What is it, exactly, that you should focus on when you look inside yourself?

Dr. Dyer: In selling, your mental focus has to be on enjoying what you're doing, finding a sense of fulfillment.

Question: In your book, *Gifts from Eykis,* you write that it is preferable to stop listening to the outside world and to begin consulting your inner voices.

Dr. Dyer: Right.

Question: Do you mean that most salespeople do not listen to their inner signals?

Dr. Dyer: Most of us are trained not to trust what we're saying to ourselves.

Question: We are unaware of the importance of self-talk and we're untrained in responding in self-enhancing ways.

Dr. Dyer: Generally, we train people to trust somebody else.

Question: How do you learn inner listening and inner responding?

Dr. Dyer: By practice, by doing it. There is no other way.

Question: In your book, you're saying, "Your mind is the captain of the ship called your body." How do you propose that people get captains' licenses?

Dr. Dyer: The only way to get that license is to begin practicing new things. You don't learn by someone else's telling you.

Question: You make it sound so easy, as if you were saying the access to our subconscious mind is as easy as dialing a toll-free number.

Dr. Dyer: It's easier, because you don't need a telephone.

Question: Let's say you're preparing for an important presentation. Before your big day, you wake up in the middle of the night because you've had a bad dream.

Dr. Dyer: You're the one who dreamed it; you take responsibility for your dreams. You can train yourself to dream or not to dream anything you want. We have all kinds of evidence to substantiate that. It's hard work to really get in tune with dreams, but I did that for one year. I recorded all my dreams. I forced myself to wake up every single night for a year just to find out what I was dreaming.

Question: So you're saying that you can use your mind more efficiently by learning how to listen to its messages.

Dr. Dyer: When you set your mind to doing something, you can do anything. It can alter your heart rate; it can rid you of diseases. There is a will in everyone that is very difficult to describe. I see it when I run a marathon—26.2 miles. Since October 6, 1977, I have not missed one day of running a minimum of eight miles. Not one single day. There is a will in everyone that doesn't come from anything that is inherited, or any electrochemical processes. It comes from the choices we make in our lives. Everything in life is a choice. I don't think it is a chemical imbalance that creates the way we think. I think it is the other way around; that is, our thinking indeed can create chemical imbalances. That's precisely what an ulcer is.

Question: One of Zig Ziglar's concepts is "garbage in, garbage out." You're saying that even if there is garbage around you, if you think happy thoughts, you could get chocolate cake out the other side?

Dr. Dyer: It may not necessarily be chocolate cake, but it's still a miracle; it's still something to appreciate. I've learned this from being around handicapped people, from having friends who are blind or deaf. People with handicaps often say, "I treat my handicap as a gift." It's not a curse; it's an opportunity. Look at some of the accounts from POWs. A POW is put in the worst conditions in the world and the thing that saves him is his mind. His crucial choice is to think in a self-enhancing rather than a self-defeating manner.

Question: I've heard comments from sales managers saying your books and tapes all sound very good. They like the promise of becoming self-actualized, but when they try to translate your ideas into everyday reality, they say it's easier said than done.

Dr. Dyer: We all keep falling down. And I do, too. I fall down all the time, but I never said that no-limit people don't fall down. It's what you do when you fall down that makes you a no-limit person.

Question: Could you give us an example of how you've fallen down and picked yourself up?

Dr. Dyer: You're talking to one of the biggest failures who ever lived. When *Erroneous Zones* came out and they told me there was no advertising budget, I said, "Well then I'll have to go out and do it myself." When they said that they couldn't distribute the book, I said, "I'll buy some; I'll take them with me." To me, that was an opportunity rather than an obstacle. If they don't have the money, then I'll have to take out a loan and do it myself. There was never a time when I said, "I guess I'll just have to give up on this." Successful people don't just land where they are on a parachute. You've got to climb up there; you've got to go through all the hurdles and look for the opportunities.

Question: Let's assume that in spite of your efforts, your book didn't sell. You lost all your money. Would you have succeeded in thinking happy thoughts?

Dr. Dyer: Sure. No question. When I got down to writing it, I never thought I'd make a nickel on it. I had been writing for five years and never made any money.

Question: Why did you write it?

Dr. Dyer: I wrote it for me. I felt that I had something to say that hadn't been said.

Question: Aren't you in a way talking like someone who has $2 million in his bank account and says making money is easy?

Dr. Dyer: I was saying the same thing when I was working as a bag boy at a supermarket in Detroit, when I was shining shoes, or driving a cab. I always had money. I grew up in an orphanage and I know about things like hunger from experience. I've never had an allowance; I've never had anybody give me a nickel in my life. Still, people think I'm talking from the perspective of a rich guy. I have been rich only a few of my years. I always had more than one job, because I didn't care for unemployment benefits or blaming the economy. I knew I had to go out and get a job. Not only did I get one, I had one in the morning, one in the afternoon, and another at night, plus going to school on top of it.

Question: What's your definition of success?

Dr. Dyer: Living your life the way you choose to, without interfering with anybody else's right to do the same.

Question: In your book, *The Sky's the Limit,* you've made the promise of becoming a no-limit person. What about delivery?

Dr. Dyer: I deliver for myself and that's all I can take responsibility for. I am an example of somebody who has come out of a family where nobody went to college. We were as poor as you can get. My parents got divorced when I was one year old; my stepfather was an abusive alcoholic. I'm saying that you don't have to use your childhood as an excuse for not growing. It is never too late to have a happy childhood. I've a sign on my mirror that says, "Maybe we can change the world if we start with ourselves." It was sent to me by someone who read one of my books. I look at it every day and I say, "Just take responsibility for yourself. Do what you can."

ABUNDANCE IN SALES

"All successful people know how to focus their minds on what they want," says Dyer. If success is what you're after, then you'd better understand that the mind is what you're all about. Dyer believes that if we focus on abundance, we will realize it, hence his book title, *You'll See It When You Believe It.* Conversely, concentrating on the negative aspects of life will produce more negativity, both in your mind and actions.

"The antecedent to every action is a thought, and what you think about expands. If you think about scarcity, convinced that you can't close a deal or that the customer will never buy, then your mind will focus on that. If you focus your mind on the negative, that's what you'll achieve. So ask yourself how much of your mind you're devoting to what you're missing. "Every problem you have you experience in your mind. The solution to the problem is in the same place, and it won't go away just because you change your external circumstances. If you want abundance, think abundance."

Dyer offers some solid tips on visualization to help you realize the results you want. Your actions, he says, come from your images, so it is critical that you choose the mental images you want. In sales situations, concentrate on the many benefits your product will bring the customers, and see them in agreement with you. Imagining a lost sale can actually precondition you for failure and set up the behaviors that lead a customer to turn you down. Forget trying to change your behavior, Dyer urges. Instead, work on those things inside your consciousness that lead to the behavior.

Second, "Tell yourself that everything you visualize is already here." The opportunity to make thought become a reality is up to you. Don't be constrained by thinking that your dreams are impossible or unrealistic. Simply act to make them happen. Finally, forget about perseverance and personal drive—they don't help you understand the visualization process or bring it into your life. Instead, recall Dyer's concept of "willingness." Be willing to do whatever it takes to achieve your dream. Often we hear those who fail say, "I gave it my best shot." What is invariably lacking, says Dyer, is their willingness to do whatever might be necessary in order to succeed. "This is the single most important aspect of visualization and imagery," says Dyer. "Everything that you can picture in your mind is already here waiting for you to connect to it. What needs to be added is your state of willingness."

You needn't climb a mountain of obstacles and work yourself to death in order to find abundance, according to Dyer. All you have to do is see what you want and be open to letting it happen. Be prepared for what you find. Abundance may amount to material wealth, or it may mean the much more satisfying riches of peace, self-assuredness, and harmony. Dyer would argue that you can't really enjoy the former without first attaining the latter. He likens the experience of reaching this state of awareness to walking through a gate into a beautiful garden. "I passed through the gate many years ago," he says with a smile. "Once you enter, there's no going back."

CHAPTER 4

DR. NORMAN VINCENT PEALE'S POSITIVE THINKING

FOR MILLIONS OF PEOPLE throughout the world, Dr. Norman Vincent Peale was "the power of positive thinking," also the title of his favorite book, which has become one of the top best sellers of all time, published in over 30 languages. Dr. Norman Vincent Peale, called the most influential Protestant clergyman in the United States, gained enduring fame as the pastor of Marble Collegiate Church, author of numerous best-selling books, editor of *Guideposts* magazine, and radio and television commentator. His distinguished career began more than 60 years ago in Ohio, when he took a job as a door-to-door salesman. In the intervening years, and until his death in the 1990s, he had become most widely recognized for his major literary contribution, *The Power of Positive*

Thinking. It is surprising to many that Dr. Peale's insights into positive thinking were developed during the years when he himself suffered from a severe lack of self-esteem. In his own words, "I was filled with self-doubt."

In this interview, Dr. Peale tells how positive thinking can be the power behind the successful salesperson. He also discusses the attitudes that lead to sales success, the techniques of positive imagination, the energy drain of negative thoughts, and how to deal with the two common factors of failure.

DR. NORMAN VINCENT PEALE: KEY IDEAS TO REMEMBER

1. You can make yourself sick with your thoughts, and you can make yourself well with them. Negative thoughts create negative emotions that take energy out of you. Positive thoughts and images create positive emotions and restore your energy.

2. You are the sovereign judge of any thought that goes through your mind. You can't stop the birds from flying over your head, but you can keep them from building a nest in your hair.

3. The only thing stronger than fear is faith.

4. A problem is a concentrated opportunity. The only people that I have ever known to have no problems are in the cemetery. Everybody I've ever known who succeeded in a big way in this life has done so by breaking problems apart and finding the values that were there.

5. Action creates motivation. Action is the best medicine I know.

Question: Is it true that you've been in the business of selling pots and pans?

Dr. Peale: That is right and I think I am still in the selling business. I see salesmanship as a process of persuasion whereby another individual is induced to walk the road of agreement with you. If I persuade you that this chair is what you want, and you agree, then you walk the road of agreement with me and you buy it. The same is true when I am in the pulpit. If I give you a concept that is going to be beneficial to you and you accept it, I have "sold" it to you, even if you do not have to pay me any money for it.

Question: You said once that many people fail in selling because they are victims of a "hardening of their thoughts and attitudes." What kinds of attitudes lead to sales success?

Dr. Peale: Let's say you're coming to sell me life insurance. You know that in order to buy groceries and clothes for your family, you need to sell so much insurance. Now, if you come in with that attitude, you convey to me—maybe unconsciously—that I've got to buy insurance from you to help you out, to do something for you. However, if you believe that you are going to help me by having the protection, the financial security, and the benefits of working with your company, that positive attitude is very likely to result in my signing the order.

Question: You once defined the word *personality* as "how you affect or stimulate others and how others affect or stimulate you." How do you prevent a customer's negative attitude from stimulating you negatively?

Dr. Peale: I once read about a meeting President Reagan was going to have with a South American president. He was told by his worried aides that this president was going to give a speech criticizing the United States. Reagan just leaned back and said with a smile, "Well, we'll smother him with love." Now, I do not particularly like the word *smother,* but when you've got a difficult customer, the thing to do is just send out goodwill thoughts, love thoughts, understanding thoughts, and remain, at all costs, dispassionate. Just take a scientific attitude and ask yourself, "Why does he act that way? There must be something disturbing him that I don't know about."

Question: It's not because of you that he's acting that way.
Dr. Peale: That's right. So you love him just the same. It's nothing personal. You just take him as he is and like him.

Question: Instead of wishing he were different?
Dr. Peale: You can't make him over. You expose a pleasant nature to him and take him as he is.

Question: So, your own attitude remains positive?
Dr. Peale: Right.

Question: You've recently written about positive imagination. How can your techniques be used in selling?
Dr. Peale: There is a deep tendency in our human nature to become ultimately almost precisely what we imagine or image ourselves as being. A customer may say, "That is very interesting, but I don't need your merchandise right now. However I will keep this in mind." Keeping it in mind

means that he will hold the image of a later purchase. Cultivation of an image is very important in selling.

Question: Images plant the seeds.

Dr. Peale: That is a good figure. Seeds will flower. While you are busy planting, you are imaging the flowers. That is the image. When you buy seeds, you are sold by the picture of the flowers on the package. Images do the selling job for you to a considerable extent.

Question: Do you think that our images and thoughts are mainly responsible for how we feel?

Dr. Peale: You can make yourself sick with your thoughts and you can make yourself well with them.

Question: So, if you think negative thoughts, you're creating negative emotions, which in turn drain your energy?

Dr. Peale: Definitely. A negative emotion creates tiredness, which takes energy and vitality out of you. A positive emotion is created by positive thoughts and images. You can say, "This is a great day. I am fortunate to sell a wonderful product. I look forward to meeting many interesting people today; I will be able to help some of these people, and they will become my friends. I look forward to learning a great deal today." Thinking and talking that way adds to your enthusiasm and vitality. Your mind is expanding, and all this contributes to your well-being.

Question: On the other hand, you could start with 100 percent energy at 9:00 in the morning and reach a 30 percent level at noon by engaging in negative thinking.

Dr. Peale: Yes, you can completely wear yourself out by the debilitating quality of your thoughts.

Question: In other words, positive thinking maintains the original energy you already have.

Dr. Peale: If you think positively, hopefully, optimistically, enjoyably, pleasantly, your words will have a therapeutic effect. If you put yourself down mentally, you are reducing the vitality of your system. I knew a doctor once who told me of a man who actually killed himself by hateful thoughts.

Question: Why is it that people can't resist thinking negative thoughts to the point of hurting themselves? Is it because they can't stop thinking these negative thoughts, or is it because they cannot imagine positive thoughts?

Dr. Peale: It requires strength of character to make the transition to a positive thinker. It isn't easy. When a person is born, he or she is a positive thinker. I've never seen a negative baby, though a baby may be born into a home where perhaps one of the parents is a negative thinker. He may listen to negative teachers, or he may be surrounded by negative friends. If that person desires to be a positive thinker, he faces a complete reversal of his mental attitude. That person will have to gradually reorganize his mind and develop new tracts across the brain. This may take some time. Some people think they can read a book and all of a sudden become positive thinkers.

Question: What would be the starting point to achieve this positive change?

Dr. Peale: Well, the realization that you are not right in your mental attitudes and that you must change would be the starting point.

Question: So, awareness would be the first step. What would be the second?

Dr. Peale: The commitment to begin practicing positive thoughts. You can develop any mental habit if you're convinced that it will lead you to success and happiness in life. Then you commit yourself to it and hang in there and stick with it and never give up.

Question: Mrs. Peale wrote in her book, *The Adventure of Being a Wife,* which is a wonderful book, "I think he writes about positive thinking because he understands so much about negative thinking."

Dr. Peale: That's right. She knows me quite well. I was indeed a negative thinker, the worst you could image. I had little faith in myself and thought that I was a failure. This was until one of my professors told me that I had a choice—that I could think positive thoughts and stop thinking negative thoughts, and that this choice would determine my future.

Question: Are you still having negative thoughts?

Dr. Peale: Sure, I have negative thoughts.

Question: Could you give us one example?

Dr. Peale: Well, yesterday was Sunday. I had to go to the church to preach a sermon. When my wife and I arrived in our garage, the attendant said, "Dr. Peale, I've got bad news for you. Your car won't start." So, I took a look at it. I got in and indeed it wouldn't start. So, we decided to take a taxi. Now, this morning, my wife asks, "What are we going to do about the car? We've got to go upstate tomorrow and the car isn't operating." I said, "I don't know what we are going to do. There is no mechanic in the garage and if we call a mechanic from the outside, he will show up next week." Here was a negative thought from the person who wrote the book, *The Power of Positive Thinking*. So, she said, "Let's believe that we're going to get that car fixed today," and she is right now with the mechanic getting it repaired. It is a good thing to have a positive-thinking wife.

Question: How can you increase your level of awareness of negative thoughts entering your mind?

Dr. Peale: I figure that I am the sovereign judge of any thought that goes through my mind. Remember the old saying, "You can't stop the birds from flying over your head, but you can keep them from building a nest in your hair." If a negative thought comes to your mind, you sit as judge with sovereign power over that thought and you can let it stay there and grow or you can cast it out. By practicing positive thinking as long as I have (being basically negative), I have developed the ability to throw out the negative thought quickly. The moment my wife said we were going to fix that car today, I agreed and ejected the negative thoughts.

Question: You seem to propose only two choices—negative thinking and positive thinking. What about realistic thinking?

Dr. Peale: The trouble is that what most people think is realistic is actually pessimistic. Look at the way newspapers write about reality. It's mostly negative. You don't find many positive thinkers on newspapers, because news is a departure from the norm. They only write about bad things that happen.

Question: Newspapers don't write about human potential.

Dr. Peale: There are very few positive publications. Our magazine, *Guideposts,* is one of the positive periodicals.

Question: You have talked about the two common factors leading to failure—inertia and aimlessness. How do you propose to deal with these?

Dr. Peale: Inertia is the difficult one. Another name for it is just plain downright laziness. It is a habit, growing in an unenthusiastic, depressed attitude of mind. Once you get into the habit of action, you'll create more enthusiastic thoughts by which to rule out inertia. Action creates motivation. Action is the best medicine I know.

Question: How about aimlessness?

Dr. Peale: If you want to avoid failure, you must develop sharp, clearly defined, enthusiastic goals: something you want to attain. I recently talked to Mr. John Johnson, the publisher of *Ebony* magazine. He was very poor and started that magazine with $600 borrowed from his grandmother. He decided he wanted to be a publisher and set small, attainable goals, one after another. Now, he not only has *Ebony,* but other magazines as well. The little goals were the starting point, but way out ahead, he had a big goal. He could see it. He imagined it.

Question: How about the problems on your way to the goals?

Dr. Peale: A problem is a concentrated opportunity. The only people that I ever have known to have no problems are in the cemetery. The more problems you have, the more alive you are. Every problem contains the seeds of its own solution. I often say, when the Lord wants to give you the greatest value in this world, he doesn't wrap it in a sophisticated package and hand it to you on a silver platter. He is too subtle, too adroit for that. He takes this value and buries it at the heart of a big, tough problem. How he must watch with delight when you've got what it takes to break that problem apart and find at its heart what the Bible calls "the pearl of the great price." Everybody I've ever know who succeeded in a big way in this life has done so by breaking problems apart and finding the value that was there.

Question: In your book, *The Power of Positive Thinking,* you mention a study saying that 75 percent of the people surveyed listed as their most difficult problem the lack of self-confidence. Do you think that is still true today?

Dr. Peale: Yes, there are so many people who have no confidence. They don't believe in themselves.

Question: Your wife wrote in her book, "Norman's creativity carried a price tag, and that price tag was a constant vulnerability in self-doubt." How did you overcome it?

Dr. Peale: I haven't overcome it. I still wonder whether I can put this speech across, and so, I say to myself, "Do you know this subject?" And I say, "Yes, I've studied it." Then I say to myself, "There is Bill Jones out there in the audience and he is going to listen to me and he thinks I know something that is going to benefit him." So I begin to fortify myself self-confidence, because of Bill Jones's faith in me. I say a prayer and then I say to myself, "Forget yourself; forget your name; don't make a big deal out of this; simply go out there, love those people, and help them."

Question: It's like with selling. You could say, "Forget about yourself, and talk about your customer's needs."

Dr. Peale: That's right. Go in there and help that customer. I tell you, I think that life is a battle from the beginning to the end. One of the biggest battles you will ever have will be with yourself.

Question: Victory over yourself seems to be the goal.

Dr. Peale: That's goal number one. Even if it takes you 90 years and you win victories, the old enemy of self-doubt sneaks up at you again and you must continue to hit him again, knock him out, and go forward. There is only one mental pattern that is stronger than fear and that is faith. So, cultivate faith and that will be your substitution for self-doubt.

Question: You've said, "American people are so nervous and high-strung that it almost makes it impossible to put them to sleep with a sermon." How do you combat stress without sacrificing success?

Dr. Peale: Stress comes from tension, worry, and anxiety. You can quiet yourself down if you just deepen your faith in God, in people, in yourself, and in the power of love.

Question: If you throw a blanket of faith over a personal problem, isn't there a possibility of covering up something that prevents you from growing?

Dr. Peale: Of course, that is always a possibility. To me, a positive thinker is a rugged soul who sees every difficulty. But he is not defeated by them because he knows that he has within his own mind the ability to understand, to define, to make judgments, and to arrive at right decisions. In addition, he has what it takes to overcome, to live with, or to reduce the problem. In a sense, he is a realist in that he sees everything straight, but is never overawed by difficulty.

Question: What is your meaning of success?

Dr. Peale: The meaning of success, in my judgment, is to be a whole person—completely in charge of yourself. It is to be someone who sees life as a wonderful opportunity, someone who goes out to do the very best he can with a positive attitude. Now, if that means being a doctor where you work 18 hours a day, but you enjoy being a doctor, you love it— whether you make much money or not—you are still a success. Some of the wealthiest people I have known have been the most unsuccessful because they were filled with worry that they wouldn't keep their money; they didn't know how to use it.

Question: So, to you, success means doing the work you enjoy doing.

Dr. Peale: Exactly. For me, it means writing books, running all over the country, making speeches. . . .

Question: One hundred years from now, how would you like to be remembered?

Dr. Peale: I'd like to be remembered as a person who helped people to be great persons.

Question: How do you define motivation?

Dr. Peale: To stimulate action to achieve a certain goal or objective. It's to bring a person alive and get him or her involved in the pursuit of an enterprise.

HOW POSITIVE ARE YOU?

Answer each of the following questions. Give yourself 10 points for each yes answer and 0 points for each no answer. Add the totals.

1. Have you had a stream of positive thoughts today?

2. Have you smiled today—before you left home?

3. Do you always maintain a positive attitude—even when you have to deal with negative people?

4. Have you helped a client or prospect with a problem during the last three days?

5. Have you read (or listened to) positive information during the past 24 hours?

6. Do you have at this moment a clearly defined, enthusiastic goal?

7. When you lose a sale, do you immediately continue building positive self-esteem?

8. Do you sincerely believe that faith is stronger than fear?

9. Have you planned for a positive, quiet moment for yourself today?

10. Do you feel that each problem contains the seed to its own solution?

Total your score. A score of 100 means that you are 100 percent positive. The difference between your score and 100 indicates the amount of thinking required for a more positive you.

Question: Who first motivated you when you were just starting out?

Dr. Peale: Well, as a boy I was very shy. I also had a pretty well-developed inferiority complex. I was filled with self-doubt. But my mother was a very dynamic motivational person. She told me, in no uncertain terms, that I must have a higher opinion of myself as a child of God.

Question: Did she always talk to you in terms of the spiritual nature of things?

Dr. Peale: Yes, she did. She told me that I could be what I wanted if I knew what I wanted to be and if I would believe in myself and in the Lord as helping me. To my mother I owe the simple notion, "You can if you think you can."

Question: Once you left your parents' influence, was there anyone else who had a motivating influence on you?

Dr. Peale: Well, I had decided that I wanted to be a newspaperman. I worked for a time on the *Ohio Morning Republican,* which is now called the *Findlay Carrier.* The editor and owner of that newspaper, Mr. Heminger, had a son named Lowell. Now these two men used to tell me (and remember I was just filled with self-doubt at that time) that I could write if I believed that I could and if I would only forget myself and become interested in the stories that lay embedded in the lives of other people.

Question: That sounds like good selling advice as well.

Dr. Peale: Yes, it certainly is. I owe these two men a great deal for that advice.

Question: Where did you work after that?

Dr. Peale: Next I went to work for the *Detroit Journal.* I worked under an editor named Grove Patterson, one of the best of that era. One day I went in to see him and I said to him, "Mr. Patterson, how are you?" He said right back, "I am terrific!" Then he said, "And if I weren't I wouldn't tell you so, because I am determined that I will be terrific." Next he said, "So should you also, because you've got a hesitant streak, and I want to see you overcome that."

Question: So he was also interested in motivating you to go beyond your own self-doubt.

Dr. Peale: That's exactly right. He told me, "You can become a good newspaperman if you think you can." And then he would send me out on rather difficult assignments to prove his theory. He helped to build up my own self-esteem, and he also taught me how to write.

Question: So the message you were getting from your mother and your mentors in the newspaper business was the same one. You can if you think you can.

Dr. Peale: It's a powerful message, and in most cases it proves to be right.

Question: And the challenging and difficult assignments you were given helped you to grow.

Dr. Peale: That's right. I remember when I went to work for Patterson, he asked, "Have you had any experience in newspaper work?" I answered, "Oh, yes, I was associate editor of my college paper." He said, "Will you please repeat after me? 'I know absolutely nothing about journalism!' " and I said, "Yessir!"

Question: And did you learn something after that?

Dr. Peale: Well, that was a valuable experience because first he wiped the slate clean and then he taught me the essentials of writing and how to reach people. He took a big sheet of white paper and put down on it just a pencil dot. Then he asked me, "What is that?" "That's a dot," I said. He said, "No, that is a period, the greatest literary device known to man. Never write past a period."

Question: That rule could apply equally well to talking and telling. Once you've made your point, stop.

Dr. Peale: It's a good rule to keep in mind in public speaking as well. He also told me, "If you can, always use a simple word instead of a complicated one. For example, use *get* rather than *procure*. And remember to always write for the ditch digger. In that way, the ditch digger and the college professor can both understand you.

Question: Have you felt these lessons were helpful even though you didn't pursue a career in journalism?

Dr. Peale: Even though I didn't continue in that field, we do have a magazine, *Guideposts,* with 4.5 million subscribers, so I got printer's ink on my fingers a long time ago and never washed it off.

Question: I remember reading about when the building housing your magazine offices burned down and you lost all your subscriber files.

Dr. Peale: That's right. The fire burned all 20,000 of our subscriber names. At the time I thought it was a disaster. But it
turned out to be a helpful and positive thing because Lowell Thomas announced on his radio show what had happened. He told about what *Guideposts* was all about and its
inspirational and motivational message, and he asked all the
subscribers to send us new information. He also asked anyone interested in such a publication to write to us as well.
The result was that we doubled our subscribers because of
that disaster.

Question: Is that hesitant streak you had in your youth still
something you have to overcome?

Dr. Peale: I've gotten it under control, but if I'm standing
backstage waiting to be introduced to an audience I still
have twinges that go through me.

Question: How do you handle that?

Dr. Peale: I say to the Lord, "Help me to forget myself and go
out there and help everybody in that audience. I know
you're going to do that." Then I go out and start talking
and pretty soon I do have a normal attitude. I don't think
one ever completely eradicates the self-doubt feelings, but
as long as you can control them, I think that is satisfactory.

Question: It sounds like if you lose yourself in the tasks, you
don't have the time or energy to think about yourself and
your doubts.

Dr. Peale: That's true. I also remember an old actor I knew in
Hollywood telling me about all of his self-doubt and inferiority feelings. He overcame these feelings by loving the

people in the audience. He described it as sending out love vibrations to the audience and to certain people in the audience, and when he started doing that his ability to perform seemed to increase.

Question: Did he give you specific ways to do that?

Dr. Peale: He said, "When you're going to speak to an audience, send out goodwill love thoughts." I was impressed with that and I have never gone onstage since without doing that. I try to embrace the whole audience with love thoughts.

Question: What advice would you give to a sales manager who has to motivate other people?

Dr. Peale: He or she has to get motivated first. It is important to believe in what you are doing, not just casually but wholeheartedly and enthusiastically. A manager has to think, sleep, and dream the job he or she is doing. He's got to believe in the potential of other people. If he builds up other people, he will build himself up. If he does that, the more he will be affected as he affects other people. I think that the greatest thing in motivation is enthusiasm and a belief in what one is doing. A manager should certainly say, "It can be done and you can do it."

Question: So the positive expectations of other people are extremely powerful.

Dr. Peale: That's a good phrase you've just used. My wife is a perfect example of what you just said. She has been a very positive motivating force in my life. She's a very busy woman herself and really runs *Guideposts* and The Foundation for Christian Living. She directs about 600 people who work for us in these two organizations. But she will almost always go with me to speaking engagements. She lets it be known that she expects me to deliver on a high level. If I don't, she tells me so, but always in a positive way. She'll say something like, "I think at this point you might have handled this matter a little more expeditiously."

Question: You mean instead of telling you to get to the point, she uses positive phrasing like "expeditiously."

Dr. Peale: That's right, and it helps me to know she is down in the audience. I know she believes I can do a good job.

Question: She motivates the motivator.

Dr. Peale: Absolutely.

Question: What techniques can salespeople use to motivate themselves?

Dr. Peale: A salesperson on the road is alone. The feeling of aloneness can siphon off his or her motivation. I think such a person can stay motivated by carrying good motivational books and tapes on business trips. By constantly saturating his mind with motivational material, he fills his mind with positive thoughts, then goes to sleep with them on his mind, and they soak into his subconscious so that when he gets up the next day he starts out positively. Then if he would say a few affirmatives, which I always like to do . . .

Question: Like what?

Dr. Peale: Such as "I feel good this morning. I am going to have a great day today." Then a salesperson might review in his mind the people he is going to be seeing that day and say, "I'm going to help Mr. Jones today." "I'm going to do something constructive for Mr. Smith." If the salesperson is religiously minded, he or she might say, "Dear Lord, you're going to be with me all day long today and you're going to help me and you're helping me now."

Question: And then . . .

Dr. Peale: And then go out and get busy! I once knew a very successful salesman named Judson Sayre who used to begin each day by saying, "Think a good day, believe a good day, get going, and make it a good day!"

Question: It sounds like you feel that self-affirmations and positive affirmations make a big difference in getting out of the doldrums.

Dr. Peale: Affirmations are one of the most powerful forms of self-direction I know. "Oh, I wish I felt better today." That's not affirmation. But if you say, "I feel good today and I thank God for it and I'm going to have a great day," your subconscious mind will listen to this strong statement and will react in a positive way. I've done this 10,000 times and I couldn't get along without it.

Question: These positive affirmations sound like a controlling influence on your emotions.

Dr. Peale: Absolutely. Affirmation is the assertion of strength and that the power inherent in you is operating.

Question: Have you seen this work in cases other than your own?

Dr. Peale: I was in India and went to dinner at the home of a very successful man who runs a large rubber business. He showed me the bookcase in his bedroom and it was a complete library of the largest and best collection of motivational and inspirational books I have ever seen. He told me that all of those books were in his mind and that by these books he had been able to build up his large business. He invited 60 top professional and business leaders to dinner, and they all told me what a fine man he was and how much everyone respected him and were inspired by him. He had gotten all of that out of books that teach positive affirmation.

Question: In summing up, if you learn how to control your attitudes, you can make yourself into a success.

Dr. Peale: That's right, attitude is very important. The wrong attitudes repel and the right ones attract.

CHAPTER 5

DR. DENIS WAITLEY: THE SEEDS OF GREATNESS

"EARLY IN MY LIFE," says Dr. Denis Waitley, author, lecturer, motivator, and expert on winning, "I learned to develop a purpose beyond myself." During his long and impressive career, he has been a principal motivator for Super Bowl athletes, was elected as chairman of the Psychology Committee for the U.S. Olympic Sports Medicine Council, and served as simulation expert for Apollo Moon Program astronauts. Waitley credits his grandmother, his father, and an eighth grade teacher with helping him develop his personal philosophy of motivation. His grandmother used to tell young Denis, "We were given life and it's our responsibility to give it purpose. Life is not accountable to you, you are accountable to life."

Waitley has been well trained to make a good accounting of himself. Today, as a national authority on high-level performance, he brings to this growing field a list of impressive credentials. He holds a doctorate in human behavior and currently serves as a visiting scholar at the University of Southern California College of Continuing Education. He is now a leading consultant to major corporations and to government and private organizations on behavior modification, goal setting, and morale enhancement. Here are just a few highlights of his extensive career:

- Bachelor of Science from U.S. Naval Academy in Annapolis
- Motivator for Super Bowl athletes
- Chairman, Psychology Committee, U.S. Olympic Sports Medicine Council responsible for performance enhancement of American Olympic athletes
- Conducted U.S. study of Chinese brainwashing techniques
- Rehabilitation coordinator for returning U.S. Vietnam prisoners of war.
- Simulation expert for Apollo Moon Program astronauts.

In addition, Dr. Waitley is the author of the all-time best-selling audiocassette album, *The Psychology of Winning*. Surprisingly, the test of this cassette program was written, as Dr. Waitley revealed in this candid interview, at a time when he was experiencing the "reality of failing." His book, *The Seeds of Greatness* (published by Fleming H. Revell), offers great insights on obtaining further achievement.

Question: You have studied the success patterns of some of the greatest achievers around the world. What are the three most common characteristics these winners share?

Dr. Waitley: The first would be high self-esteem, the feeling of your own worth. The second, the realization that you have the responsibility for choosing your own destiny. The healthiest, most successful people I've seen exercise their privilege to choose. The power of choosing their destinies puts them in charge of their lives. The third characteristic would be creative imagination to translate dreams into specific goals.

Question: What is your definition of a winner?

Dr. Waitley: A winner is, in my opinion, an individual who is progressively pursuing, and having some success at reaching, a goal that he has set for him- or herself—a goal that is attained for the benefit, rather than at the expense, of others.

Question: In doing the research for our interview, I found that there are over 220 books that deal with the subject of winning and only 16 that deal with the subject of losing. Do you think that there is an overemphasis on winning?

Dr. Waitley: The idea of winning has been misunderstood and overexposed. It's associated with flying through airports, driving fast cars, or standing over a fallen adversary. I've seen salesmen and saleswomen who were making six-figure incomes thinking that they had won. They thought winning was reaching a certain financial level or getting to a certain point. Thinking they have arrived, they stand still and go to the country club. Now their company expects more production, but won't get it from them because they had the wrong idea. They didn't realize that winning is a continual process of improvement.

Question: In 1976, two researchers, Thomas Tutko and William Burns, published a book titled *Winning Is Everything and Other American Myths.* They wrote: "Winning, in fact, is like drinking saltwater; it will never quench your thirst. It is an insatiable greed. There are never enough victories, never enough championships or records. If we win, we take another gulp and have even greater fantasies."

Dr. Waitley: It is true. The American version of winning is to come in first at all costs, or expediency rather than integrity.

Question: Are you saying that people tend to get obsessed with winning at the expense of fulfillment?

Dr. Waitley: Definitely. I think athletics is the most dominant of all fields where payoff only comes to the winner, but there are notable exceptions. For example, in interviews with the five U.S. former Olympic decathlon winners, I found that their goal was to become the best they could, not necessarily the best in the world. These athletes have found fulfillment in recognizing and in realizing their potential.

Question: Their gold medals are internal, not external.

Dr. Waitley: Exactly. The secret is to compare yourself against a standard that you have set. You measure yourself only against your last performance, not against another individual's.

Question: What is your definition of a loser?

Dr. Waitley: A loser is a person who has an abundance of opportunities to learn, who has successful role models everywhere, but who chooses not to try. I read the other day that only 10 percent of all Americans will ever buy or read a book. This means that 90 percent choose not to take advantage of the tremendous opportunities available to everyone

SOURCES OF MOTIVATION

"Motivation doesn't only come from inside," explains Denis Waitley. For him it also comes from his family—from his wife, who is his best friend, and his children. "In our business, we travel a lot," Waitley explains. "If you're out there traveling every day, what keeps you going? Obviously if you keep your eye on the goal, you can get through anything, but just getting through is only having a destination. I have realized that you need someone to smell the roses with. Even if the roses are planted in fertilizer, you need someone to help you grow, to share experiences, to care. Beyond that, I have my faith in God. That carries me through anything. I've learned to say 'Try me' rather than 'Why me?' "

Waitley spends a lot of time reading the stories of other people who have overcome great obstacles and made contributions. He would rather look at the heroic efforts of thousands who are always struggling to build or rebuild than watch the destructive news account of how many were killed in the latest tornado or earthquake. It's the planting and the replanting efforts—all those constructive energies—that interest Denis Waitley and give him a source for optimism and the deep commitment to go on motivating others to success.

in this country. Our libraries are crammed full with enough information for anyone to be an expert in anything.

Question: Do you feel salespeople don't read enough?
Dr. Waitley: To me, the person who chooses not to read is more of a loser than the person who cannot read. I am not suggesting you need to be an intellectual in order to sell; I

am just suggesting that if you want to move up, you definitely need the additional vocabulary.

Question: You wrote in your book *The Winner's Edge,* "Real success in life has no relationship to a gifted birth, talent or IQ." Would you include gender?
Dr. Waitley: Yes, and I would include race as well.

Question: Whether you are a saleswoman or a salesman, it doesn't make a difference?
Dr. Waitley: It doesn't make a difference. In fact, there are advantages to both.

Question: What do you see as a woman's edge in selling?
Dr. Waitley: A woman has the edge of being more gifted earlier in the area of verbal communication. She has a better grasp of nonverbal signals and she is able to show more empathy in recognizing customer needs. Women are more process-oriented. Society, however, has positively conditioned a man to believe that the world is his oyster, and he's been taught to risk in order to get rewards. Women have been taught to seek security. I think women need to be more risk-oriented to create security. I also think that men need to learn how to listen more before taking risks.

Question: You have analyzed many winners. I wonder how we can ever know objectively how and why winners win.
Dr. Waitley: I don't think we can put it into a formula. But we can study people who have overcome obstacles in their paths. I studied people from every walk of life, like hostages, POWs, astronauts, sports figures, and sales achievers to see if they have anything in common. There are surprising similarities.

GETTING THE RIGHT PERSPECTIVE

"Most people always ask, 'Why me? Why do I have to go through this?' That's the wrong perspective. The right perspective is, 'What can I learn, develop, experience, share—how can I grow from this?' Then you discover that you can only scratch the surface in a lifetime. This gives me tremendous optimism and compassion and the ability to adapt. I can adapt to any situation with this philosophy. I feel compassion with others because I know that they are going through the same search for meaning. The optimism comes from the fact that we were given life and we're accountable to it. We have to account for the reasons and provide the meaning. Life has been given to us—therefore it doesn't owe us anything. People without this philosophy tend to be self-oriented, they don't treasure the internal values, and they are bound to experience a lot of frustration and depression."

Question: Let me rephrase my question. Look at history as an example. The country who wins the war gets to write the history books. History becomes the tale of the winner. If you translate this to people, winners get to tell their stories in interviews. Winners are the most interviewed people in this country. Do you think that they give us an objective picture? Is high performance an objective science or a speculative science?

Dr. Waitley: It's a speculative science. But instead of comparing their methods on achieving success, we need to compare patterns of achievement and see how those patterns overlap. Also, we need to review their thoughts and actions during their worst times. Personally, I've learned more from the worst times than I have from the best moments of my life.

Question: Do you suggest that the strength of winners often depends on how they manage disappointment?

Dr. Waitley: Absolutely. When I studied the adversities faced by leaders like Anwar Sadat, Abraham Lincoln, Walt Disney, Thomas A. Edison, and Golda Meir, I learned much more than by analyzing some of the great statements or decisions they made. When winners stand on the pedestal, they tend to gloss over what it took to get from the dream to reality.

Question: Why?

Dr. Waitley: It's a human tendency to gloss over the difficulties and remember only the great breakthroughs. Many sales executives focus on the gloss and overlook the real opportunities.

Question: How can we learn from our disappointments in a way that enhances our growth?

Dr. Waitley: Most people never go beyond the adolescent view of failure. They say, "If they laugh at me, it isn't worth learning from the experience." Adolescents tend to believe that performance is the same as the performer. They take individual achievements as marks of their own self-esteem. The healthy individual views failure as a temporary setback. The stumbling block becomes the stepping-stone. A better example would be the kid who got new ice skates for Christmas. He goes out on the ice and falls on his head. His mother comforts him by saying, "Why don't you come in and put your skates away," and he says "Mom, I didn't get my skates to fail with; I got my skates to learn with. What I'll do is keep practicing until I know how to do it right."

Question: Disappointment seems to lead up to a choice between seeking comfort and seeking solutions.
Dr. Waitley: Exactly.

Question: We are reluctant to grow and seek solutions because it's painful.
Dr. Waitley: Right; 80 percent of all people view growing pain as too uncomfortable or unacceptable; only 20 percent recognize it as a learning experience.

Question: Could you give us an example of people who view pain as a learning experience?
Dr. Waitley: Well, during the 1980 Olympics I worked with Australian Eight Olympic Rowers. The problem was that they experienced muscle spasms near the finish line. The coach told me that when they got from a 60-stroke per minute cadence up to 64 strokes per minutes, the pain was nearly unbearable. It appeared like a no-win situation. So we developed an appreciation and understanding for the process of pain as being a growth experience. Pain tells you that the muscles are working and also that you are in the peak-performance mode, which means that you are on your way to victory. We made the interesting discovery that the mind will block the pain as long as there is a positive expectation. By recognizing pain as being their friend, they ended the race without muscle spasms and they improved their performance significantly. Their minds, motivated by posi-

FEEDING BODY AND MIND

Waitley recommends regular physical activity to stay motivated. He scuba dives, power walks, swims, rides a bike, deep-sea fishes, and snow skis. But the body is not the only part of the human machine that needs a workout. "Don't use all of the energies you have to achieve," cautions Waitley, "use some of your imagination for more childlike things like making a paper airplane or kite, or entering a frisbee contest. This teaches you how to be wide open to the world. That way you'll never get in a rut. I also plan for some good, quality thinking and planning time everyday."

Waitley believes that time is the only equal-opportunity employer. He advises salespeople and managers to take walking breaks instead of talking breaks. Instead of having a speaker come to impart wisdom to a passive audience, Waitley suggests conducting brainstorming sessions where meeting participants develop new ideas.

"Get them thinking," advises Waitley. "Instead of motivating them, let them motivate you." Waitley also suggests choosing a new environment and then listening to a different tape every week, discussing its content, reviewing what they've learned, and how to apply it to their businesses.

tive expectations, released powerful endorphins that killed the pain.

Question: In your book, *The Seeds of Greatness,* you suggest that the so-called motivators preach too much about attitudes without linking them with aptitudes. What if you have great dreams for winning and a high tolerance for pain, but lack the basic talents to realize those dreams?

Dr. Waitley: I was cautioned by my friends, Dr. Jonas Salk and Hans Selye, not to tell people that they could walk on water. Why build up gigantic expectations in people without knowing what their real talents are? To shorten the answer, and I said this in the book, we now have specific and reliable tests available to assess 32 areas of natural, basic talents, like the ability to carry a tune or the ability to put tweezers together on a minute object.

Question: Who conducts these tests?

Dr. Waitley: There is a nonprofit organization, The Johnson-O'Connor Research Foundation, a human engineering laboratory with offices in major cities throughout the United States. They are headquartered in New York City.

Question: Your father did not seem to have an appreciation of your talents when he expected you to become an Annapolis graduate.

Dr. Waitley: He appreciated my talents, but tried to apply them to his own dreams. I wanted to write the great American novel and ended up as a carrier-based attack jet pilot.

Question: So, you are saying that before people can reach their true potential, they need to discover their true talents?

Dr. Waitley: Yes. In my seminars, I ask the audience, if they could live their lives over again, what would they do? Eighty percent of them say that they would be doing something else.

Question: In your book *The Winner's Edge* you said, "I didn't realize until I was 35 that I am behind the wheel in my life."
Dr. Waitley: That's right.

Question: What made you aware of that?
Dr. Waitley: I was failing a lot up until 35.

Question: At what were you failing?
Dr. Waitley: I became a good navy pilot, but I never became the astronaut that I wanted to be. That, to me, was a failure. I could fly a plane, but I didn't get to fly a spaceship. Later, as a business executive, I earned an income, but never retained my money. I had a couple of business failures. I fixed the blame on my father's suggestion to go the Naval Academy. I rationalized, what can an ex-navy pilot do except fly for an airline?

Question: You thought that your opportunities were limited?
Dr. Waitley: Yes. Then I figured that I had never learned anything about money. I know a lot about words, so I took several staff positions. I began to see myself as a jack-of-all-trades and a master of none. People told me "Denis, you are one of the most gifted, talented, creative, wonderful individuals we ever met. We are sure sorry you have not been able to convert that to financial or any other lasting success." At 35, I probably was at the lowest point in my life. I had been traveling all the time. I didn't have a good family life. My resume looked like Who's That? instead of Who's Who, and I was actually believing that I might be born to lose. Like my dad, because he never made any money either. Interestingly enough, and I don't think he would mind my

saying this, a best-selling author today, a friend of mine, said as we were walking on the beach that he had the same experience. Until he realized that his dreams had substance and until he started simulating success and being around people who were successful, he was destined, as I, to have permanent potential. Then his book became a big *New York Times* best seller.

Question: What is his name?
Dr. Waitley: Spencer Johnson, the coauthor of *The One-Minute Manager.*

Question: So you walked on the beach, wondering if your dreams were realistic or not?
Dr. Waitley: Some of my dreams were pipe dreams. Becoming an astronaut was unrealistic. I recognized that these unattainable dreams led to repeated failures.

Question: What did you do to get out of this failure pattern?
Dr. Waitley: I happened to get fed up with the repeating cycle. I began to seek shelter under the shade of winners. I got tired of running with the turkeys. The first thing that I did was to find a very strong clergyman. I needed some real fatherly advice. We did go up 10,000 feet in an airplane. He knew flying was a comfortable environment, a success pattern for me. As we were going through the stalls and spins, he gave me reassurance and spiritual dimension at a time when I needed it most. The second thing I did was start going to seminars conducted by high-powered professionals who talked about stress, health, and success. I was studying their patterns of success. I got excited that

maybe I was going to be acceptable in this kind of company. When things were at their worst, I began to write *The Psychology of Winning.*

Question: So at the lowest point of your life, you actually created the biggest sales hit in the cassette market. How did your program come to be published?

Dr. Waitley: I think Earl Nightingale and Lloyd Conant are the only two who know this, but after I'd finished *The Psychology of Winning,* I took my last $500 and flew to Chicago. At that time I was speaking in churches, getting less than $50 a speech. Someone who believed in me had sent a single cassette, which I'd recorded in church, to Earl Nightingale. He called me and told me that he liked my voice and thought I had some good ideas. He said if I were ever in Chicago, I should see his partner, Lloyd Conant. I went on the next airplane, and Lloyd Conant believed in my work enough to help me polish up my initial draft and took a chance on recording *The Psychology of Winning,* which literally converted me from almost total anonymity to a certain measure of success.

Question: Now that you've met with success, do you feel an overabundance of success can spoil us?

Dr. Waitley: Absolutely. If you put . . . the approving crowd, the amount of money you make, and the material accomplishments into a bag and say that is success, you would be making a big mistake.

Question: What are the danger signals of success? When you know that you are not riding success, but success is riding you?

Dr. Waitley: There are several telltale signals. Number one is an obsession to talk about your own accomplishments all the time. Two, whenever people tell you something about what they did, you top them. The third thing is an obsession with your own material rewards—a tendency to show them more. You invite people to see the monuments that you've collected.

Question: In your new book, you suggest that trying to collect life is a self-defeating proposition.

Dr. Waitley: Yes. We can't collect life; we can only celebrate life.

Question: But if we examine your journey to success, we could say that before we can celebrate, we need to manage our disappointments.

Dr. Waitley: I really believe so. We've got to view failures and rejections as healthy experiences from which to grow. We've got to replace "someday" fantasies with goals that we can really track and chip away at every day. We've got to let go of our impossible dreams and stop putting happiness and success on layaway.

Question: I'd like to share an interesting quote with you. Abraham Zaleznik wrote in a *Harvard Business Review* article titled "Managing Disappointment," "There is irony in all of human experience. The deepest irony of all is to discover that one has been mourning losses that were never sustained and yearning for a past that never existed, while ignoring one's own real capabilities for shaping the present."

Dr. Waitley: That is really profound and is said so well. Because planting the seeds of greatness means investing your natu-

THE POWER OF VISUALIZATION

Denis Waitley's most motivating experience happened one day in 1964 as he looked out from his office as a part-time manager of a small-time golf course. He was making about $600 a month, was in between jobs, and had recently left the navy. He says he did not know what he was going to do with his life. "I remember I slipped off into this marvelous daydream visualizing myself on the course with a badge on, standing on the eighteenth hole with the crowd lining up for a PGA tournament. It was a great event. I saw Jack Nicklaus coming up, and then Arnold Palmer, and I saw the title of executive director on my badge with TV cameras from ABC—the whole works. I saw myself as the originator of this great golf event.

"But here I was on this little golf course with no country club. Without releasing myself from that dream, I reached over and called Burbank and asked if I could speak to Andy Williams. I figured if Bob Hope and Bing Crosby had a tournament, and since Andy Williams was at the peak of his career at that time, why not try? I was at the peak of my confidence, and I got through to him. I believe that something in my voice must have come across and he said, 'If you ever put together a deal like you're describing, I'd consider it.' Four years later, the Salk Institute with Dr. Jonas Salk was the beneficiary of millions of dollars from the first Andy Williams Golf Tournament in San Diego. The motivating experience of that creative daydream led me to all that."

Denis Waitley has the phenomenal ability to capture the currents running through himself, and, more important, he takes the time to listen to his inner voices. A lot of motivation comes from listening to yourself, knowing yourself, and from letting your inner voice speak. "Yes," says Waitley, "the inner listening shows you the beauty that is available."

ral talents in the pursuit of realistic goals. Not every seed will grow into a flower, so you need to view these failures as learning experiences. But to enjoy the flowers in your garden, you have to pluck the weeds. This means that you have to recognize and give up your pipe dreams.

Question: And if you don't?
Dr. Waitley: Your natural seeds of greatness will never have an opportunity to bloom.

CHAPTER 6

TOM HOPKINS ON MASTERING THE ART OF MOTIVATION

❧———————❧

GREAT SALESPEOPLE must have at heart the interests of their customers, for no business can develop except as it promotes the interests of those who use its goods or its services. In selling, the greatest possible unselfishness is the most enlightened selfishness. For most sales professionals, experience has taught that the effort to make a person buy something he or she does not need in the long run defeats its own purpose. Supersalespeople will not only study the immediate needs of their customers, but will provide against those needs even before customers realize that they exist.

One of the greatest elements of skill in a salesperson is to create in the customer's mind the thought that the salesperson's company will be able to produce the goods that the salesperson is trying to sell. The samples may be fine, but the customer must know that the people in the factory behind the samples will also do their part to the uttermost. Great salespeople must be those, furthermore, who cannot only make the customer want to buy, but who can also make their own producing organization equally enthusiastic to deliver the goods. This is something new in salesmanship.

Good salesmanship means getting a good price for good material. The best salesperson is not always the one who sells the greatest quantity at the best price.

Success in selling is largely a matter of personal integrity well directed. Unless you can sell yourself, you will never have the opportunity to sell something else. And the biggest possible personal selling point is integrity. Therefore, it is important to cultivate integrity; cultivate and cherish and develop it.

If you are in a line of work that does not give you pleasure, you are wrongly placed and you had better start afresh. Go to that which you delight to do and you must succeed. Be sure that you bend over backward in your endeavor to establish a reputation for honesty and right doing.

Supersalespeople are true to the interests of the customer. Your supreme purpose is to quicken the customers' imagination and make them see the true virtues of the goods that you are selling to them. "I learned a long time ago," says ultrasuccessful sales trainer, best-selling author, and motivator Tom Hopkins, "that selling is the highest-paid hard work and the lowest-paid easy work I could find. I also learned that the choice was all mine." Hopkins decided on the hard-work path, and his efforts have paid off handsomely for himself and for the thousands upon thousands he has helped to do the same. On average, he trains about 100,000 salespeople a year in the United States and abroad, while he earns a cool $10,000 every time he sets foot on stage to do his thing.

What he does is worth it. Covering every conceivable aspect of selling, from Applied Presentation Skills to Closing Zeal, Hopkins mottoes, "Money is good" and "Champions love people and use money, not the other way around," are like rally-style initiation rites. "My goal," explains Hopkins, "is to change the image that most people have of the salesman who just wants to cram his product down the prospect's throat. The average American today is more sophisticated, and wants to buy from someone with understanding and warmth. No one wants to be sold," he goes on philosophically, "but they do want to own things."

In Hopkins's view, salespeople can relate to him because, no matter how many downs they may have had, he has had at least as many, maybe more. "Self-motivation is one of the salesperson's most important tools," he claims, explaining, "There is no substitute for product knowledge and sales technique, but without a positive self-image, all is lost." Hopkins believes that salespeople in particular must learn to benefit from adversity and failure. He sums up what he has learned about success by saying, in characteristically positive tones, "I am not judged by the number of times I fail, but by the number of times I succeed. And that is in direct proportion to the number of times I can fail and keep on trying."

Question: How do you define motivation?

Tom Hopkins: To me, motivation is the ability to get people to stretch further than they are accustomed to in order to reach their goals.

Question: Is motivation the same for everyone?

Tom Hopkins: No. Motivation is different for different types of people. Some people are self-motivated. They have the ability to reach within themselves for the strength to do what they really don't want to do but may have to do in order to reach their desired goals.

Question: What are some of the other types of people?

Tom Hopkins: There are others who need someone on a periodic basis to sit down with them and review their goals and achievements and to give them praise and recognition to further motivate them. Then you also have a certain number of people who don't want to change. Motivation for them becomes a negative force.

Question: How do you mean that?

Tom Hopkins: You cannot change people who do not want to change. You can only effect a change in someone who is ready for it. If you try to change someone who is not ready, they will resist, producing a counterproductive force to motivation. They will use all their energies in a negative way.

Question: Would you agree that people who do not want to change will get shortchanged?

Tom Hopkins: Yes, I would. I also find that people have to be at a certain point in their lives. The ones who have done their best in a self-motivated environment have something to prove to somebody, even if that person is the individual himself.

Question: In your view, what do they have to prove?

Tom Hopkins: They have a tremendous desire to either prove themselves to others or to themselves, or to accomplish something they haven't done before. They have an innate need to grow beyond their present parameters.

Question: Who motivated you at the beginning of your career?
Tom Hopkins: I think I fall right into that category we just talked about—I had something to prove.

Question: To yourself?
Tom Hopkins: Both to myself and to my father. He wanted me to be a famous attorney and I lasted for only 90 days in college. When I quit, I came home to tell my father and he was very disappointed and said, "I will always love you even though you'll never amount to anything."

Question: How did you feel about that?
Tom Hopkins: To me, this was a tremendous emotional and psychological motivator because I told myself, "Okay, I'm going to prove I can become a success."

Question: How did you accomplish that goal?
Tom Hopkins: I went into construction, and although I was making a pretty decent wage at the age of 17, I still wasn't satisfied. At 18, I decided to try sales. Even there I had a problem. I had to take the real estate exam twice.

Question: What was your motivation at that time?
Tom Hopkins: I wanted to win. If there was any kind of a contest, say for a trophy, that meant more to me than the money. If there was a vacation contest, I went after that. And then, all of a sudden, my life became a series of little victories because I began to win—to reach my goals.

Question: Was there a big growth step that happened at some point?

Tom Hopkins: In 1968 I set a goal to sell more homes than anyone else had ever sold in one year. When I reached that goal, I started thinking about management.

Question: How do you sum up the effects of this desire to prove something?

Tom Hopkins: If a person doesn't have something to prove, or doesn't have a tremendous need or desire, it's easy to just coast along.

Question: Your example with your father is a good one. Did he use that same technique to motivate you when you were younger?

Tom Hopkins: He started out like a lot of parents. He always would say that if I didn't get a degree I wouldn't amount to anything. He was kind of a perfectionist.

Question: So he would exert a slight pressure by informing you of the consequences of a certain action or lack of it?

Tom Hopkins: Sure. The greatest motivator is either the fear of losing something or of having something bad happen to you. A lot of good managers use fear properly to motivate people.

Question: Who or what motivates you now?

Tom Hopkins: Well, now I feel almost an obligation to help other people realize their goals. We're all motivated by different things—money, achievement, recognition, security, acceptance of others, love of family, self-acceptance, or becoming our own person, and feeling satisfied with life.

Question: What demotivates people?

Tom Hopkins: People who are demotivated are suffering from things like self-doubt. They may fear that they won't be able to achieve their goals, or they may be listening to negative voices from outside themselves. This can affect a person's mind and attitude.

Question: So fear of failure can be a demotivator?

Tom Hopkins: Yes. Some people are so afraid of failing that they won't even try. They've been defeated before they attempt anything—defeated by their own lack of confidence or loss of sense of security. They won't take any risk at all, and the last step of demotivation is the immobilization that comes from their inability to change.

Question: For many people there has been a significant experience with or because of some hero who has been a motivating factor. Did you have a hero who motivated you?

Tom Hopkins: Yes, I did. His name was J. Douglas Edwards. I consider him to have been the father of American selling. When I was 19, I spent the last $150 I had to go to a five-day training that he was conducting.

Question: Why did you decide to do that?

Tom Hopkins: Well, you see, I had failed miserably when I started in selling. It goes back to the fact that I hadn't had any training. Now, J. Douglas Edwards's intensive five-day training literally taught me what I call the art of closing the sale.

Question: And what did you learn?

Tom Hopkins: I learned all the steps to go through to qualify a prospect and sell the product.

Question: Did Edwards's course make a great difference in your professional life?

Tom Hopkins: Yes, it did, and he became my hero. I found that I wanted to become a top producer and I also wanted to earn his esteem. He became one of the main forces in my life.

Question: And later in your life were there other motivating forces?

Tom Hopkins: After Edwards, I really didn't have another hero for a long time. But I read an enormous amount—authors like Dr. Norman Vincent Peale and Zig Ziglar. These people have really done such a tremendous job for the world. I studied the art of selling, and, after I sold the real estate office I had managed, I decided that I wanted to teach. It's been very motivating working to help others realize their goals the way Edwards helped me realize mine.

Question: What suggestions do you have for sales managers or trainers who want to motivate others to realize their goals?

Tom Hopkins: I think the first important step is to help other people set their own goals. These goals have to be better than what the person is currently doing, but they still have to be believable.

Question: How does the manager do that?

Tom Hopkins: Well, every manager should sit down with a new salesperson and ask him or her questions right in the beginning; not just talk, but actually ask specific questions, such as "I'd like you to answer some questions—would you like me to help you reach your goal?" And then, "Let's outline a couple of goals that would make you happy—what kind of a car would you really like to have in the next year or two?" And the manager should write that down in this salesperson's folder. They should do it together and then outline other goals, like the kind of house this salesperson might want to be living in over the next two or three years and so on.

Question: How many goals should the manager help the salesperson set?

Tom Hopkins: I think about five or six. Other goals would include what income for the first year's work would make the salesperson feel he or she had done a really good job. Get the salesperson to commit himself to specific and measurable goals, and make the two of you partners in that effort.

Question: What would you do then?

Tom Hopkins: Then I would ask, "Do you want me to help you reach those goals?" I would get a commitment.

Question: Is there a step after the commitment?

Tom Hopkins: Yes, you must get that person's permission, an indication that he or she is ready to have you help him reach those goals in very specific ways by showing him what he is doing right and wrong—by helping him improve his professional performance. That's the tough part. You say, "If need be, would you allow me to sit down with you and make suggestions, critique and advise you on what you need to do to reach the goals we've just outlined?"

Question: You got permission to act as a mentor?

Tom Hopkins: Yes, and also as a disciplinarian if necessary. I then go a step further. I think the manager has to write down two agreements. One is, "I hereby agree to do whatever is necessary to help John Smith reach the outlined goals." Then I sign my name. Then I ask John Smith to write down that he agrees to let me do whatever is necessary to help reach those goals.

Question: So you make a countercommitment to the goals that you've set together?

Tom Hopkins: That's right. Now, if John Smith is sitting around down in the dumps three months later, the manager can say, "Look, you're not making enough calls and contacting enough people. You've got to do more prospecting." Now both the salesperson and the manager are interdependent and have made a commitment, in writing, to work together, so it's unlikely that the salesperson is either going to resent the manager's advice or feel threatened by it. He is more likely to act on it and to succeed in his profession.

Question: So a good manager acts as a guide, a disciplinarian, a mentor, and a teacher?

Tom Hopkins: That's the way I see the manager's role. But also, a manager should do some research into the past of the new salesperson. He or she should know what that salesperson was making before and what he already has in terms of lifestyle. Most people don't make drastic lifestyle changes. If someone is driving a $10,000 car and says he wants to be driving a $40,000 car in a year, the manager's role is to help that person define a more realistic goal that is reachable and reasonable, and maybe put the higher goal down the road a few years. Most people grow gradually, and that's healthy.

Question: How about the superstar who comes in and really outperforms all the manager's expectations?

Tom Hopkins: That happens, but it's only about one in a thousand. For the rest of the salespeople out there, goals that are unrealistic can lead to a despondent attitude, and that's very demotivating.

Question: Big fantasies can end up in big disappointments?

Tom Hopkins: Yes. You've got to have a work plan, and the best time to complete it is the night before. That way you'll wake up motivated and you won't be floundering around for half a day just defining what you want to accomplish.

Question: What would be another technique?

Tom Hopkins: Don't get in a rut. I tell people to vary their routines—maybe not to wake up at the same time every day, not to drive the same way to work or to their territory. In other words, don't confine yourself. New things to look at and new ways of doing things lead to new ideas, and new ideas lead to an expanded horizon. Expanding your horizons automatically leads to bigger success.

Question: What do you do to stay motivated in your own life?

Tom Hopkins: I am a strong believer that you have to live what you teach. I do all the things we've talked about here. Plus, I believe, as they say in show business, the show must go on. If I've flown from one time zone to another and I'm tired, I still go ahead as planned, and I find that once you get up there in front of people who are looking to you for help, you have to give the best you've got. When you're giving your best, say as a salesperson talking with a customer, and you're not feeling that good, you start faking it and suddenly you're actually making it. Your adrenaline kicks in and you really do feel good, and you're doing a good job.

Question: What do you think about the negative aspects of selling—like rejection?

Tom Hopkins: You can't take rejection personally. That's the cardinal rule. The only way you can manage your feelings about rejection is to change your attitude toward the word *no*. If you have to talk to five people to get one order, and you earn $100 every time you get an order, then each *no* is worth $25, because out of five you'll get four noes and one yes. Instead of getting depressed each time you hear no, you say thanks for the $25 and make the next call.

Question: Do you teach any other mental attitude boosters?

Tom Hopkins: I ask students of my courses to memorize certain things like: "I never see failure as a failure but only as a learning experience." Or, "I never see failure as failure but only as the negative feedback I need to change course in my direction."

Question: What do you call these?

Tom Hopkins: I call them the "attitude toward failure."

Question: Are there others?

Tom Hopkins: Yes. "I never see failure as a failure but only as the opportunity to develop my sense of humor, or only as part of a game I must play to win." The last is, "Selling and business and life are all a big percentage game."

Question: What was your most demotivating experience?

Tom Hopkins: When I was just starting out I sold four homes, all contingent on one of them going to a close. I worked for three months on that transaction. They all fell through and I made nothing, absolutely zero.

Question: Then what happened?

Tom Hopkins: After my second year, my income started to increase and things began to improve. I changed strategy. I started to train others, and the challenges got bigger and I was able to meet them with success.

Question: What was your most motivating experience?

Tom Hopkins: Oh, when my book, *How to Master the Art of Selling,* hit the best-seller list, without a doubt.

Question: Why was that such a great thing for you?

Tom Hopkins: Well, when I dropped out of college after 90 days, and then wrote a book that people thought worthwhile enough to buy so many copies that it hit the best-seller list, that was really motivating. Then I was invited to speak in front of 150 college professors about how to motivate students—a college dropout speaking about motivating students. I did a three-hour session on how to help students out of a study slump. I wrote the whole session for the professors. To have them sit there and take notes and then give me a standing ovation when I was done was the highlight of this college dropout's life so far.

Question: So for you, motivation comes from helping other people to grow?

Tom Hopkins: I had 10 or 15 letters recently from people who went out and increased their incomes after going through one of my courses, but I had one letter in particular. A woman wrote that she had just come out of the hospital after suffering a stroke. Half her body is paralyzed, but she went out after the course and in the first year made almost $50,000. Stories like that motivate me to spend 95 percent of my time traveling from seminar to seminar teaching my students how to become champions.

Question: What is your measure of success?

Tom Hopkins: My measure of success is to reach fulfillment in four areas. Number one is financial accomplishments, based on my own self-image and goals. Number two is emotional stability and the ability to control emotional handicaps in my own life. Number three is physical fitness and feeling good physically. And number four is maintaining my spiritual awareness and my personal relationship with a higher power. If you can do all four of these, you're a successful human being by my measure of success.

Question: There's always a tendency to go out of those bounds every day.

Tom Hopkins: Certainly, and it's a constant struggle, isn't it?

PART 2

REACH FOR THE SKY

*Surefire Strategies to
Keep You Motivated and
on Track for Success*

CHAPTER 7

DESTINED FOR SUCCESS

❧────────❧

Motivational Experts and Top Sales Performers
Weigh In on What It Takes to Send
Your Achievement Levels Soaring

INSPECT THE AVERAGE SALES rep's shelves, backseat, or file cabinet and you're bound to run across an assortment of cassettes, books, pamphlets, and other paraphernalia dedicated to one subject—achieving success. Salespeople are legendary for building veritable arsenals of motivational materials. Yet despite absorbing the collected wisdom of many of the nation's top success gurus, the average sales rep remains just that: average.

Why is it that so many sales professionals become stifled in their achievement levels or plateau before reaching the rarefied air of success they aspire to? Part of the problem, experts agree, is that too frequently people define success exclusively in financial terms, while giving short shrift to the other critical dimensions that make up a successful life. This focus is generally supported by many of our cultural values—consider how often we hear revelations of the disastrous private lives of otherwise successful business professionals or celebrities.

As a result, explains Dr. Jan Gault, psychologist and author of *The Mighty Power of Your Beliefs,* people who operate within such a narrow definition of success often find themselves ill-equipped to handle financial setbacks.

"Say you have a string of rejections, you lose a big sale, or you have to file for bankruptcy," she says. "You're going to feel like a failure if you're just hanging success on that one dimension of your life. If we can't put these unwanted outcomes into perspective with the rest of our lives and values— family, health, personal relationships, and so forth—this can throw us into a state of depression."

Gault adds that, while we don't always control outcomes and economic conditions, we do always have control over how we perceive and interpret these outcomes. "That's why our definitions of success are critical, for our mental health as well as for our ongoing success," she says.

CURB YOUR DOGMA

Noah St. John, an inspirational speaker and the author of *Permission to Succeed: Unlocking the Mystery of Success Anorexia,* argues that many people have been misled by the traditional success dogma that offers overly simple answers to complex issues. He says that when he criticizes some of the sacred cows of success literature he often taps into a wellspring of disaffection with the strategies that have proven fruitless for many.

"One thing I work hard at," he says, "is to take the clichés we hear all the time and go underneath them. One is 'Persistence is the key to success.' Well, what does that mean? Where does persistence come from? What is it? Another one we frequently hear is 'You've got to set your goals.' Well, why is that? And when I get in front of people and say these things they start nodding to themselves saying, 'Yeah, that's what I've been wondering, too.' Relying on these clichés to motivate you is like depending on Snickers bars for nutrition—they give you a lot of energy, but only briefly. That's why people walk out of motivational seminars all pumped up, but pretty soon the system breaks down, and they're left without anything to keep them going for the long haul."

WHAT'S YOUR PURPOSE?

Few would dispute that persistence and goal setting play a role in achieving success, particularly in sales. But instead of focusing on goals and persistence as the primary factors leading to success, Gault suggests beginning at the true source—a sense of purpose.

"People need to be clear about their purpose in life," she says. "Your purpose is what you feel compelled to do or to accomplish, and it's what keeps you on course. It's what gives meaning and direction to your life. So the first step is not to come up with a string of goals, but to clarify your purpose and then get more specific. Everyone should have a personal mission statement. Your goals need to be consistent with that purpose, otherwise you're not going to have the passion and enthusiasm to go out and achieve the goals you've set for yourself."

PERFORMANCE ISSUES

For more than 25 years, Dr. Kenneth Christian has been studying the problem of underachievement among people of all ages, races, and educational backgrounds. While he admits that there are frequently a variety of obstacles that keep people from achieving up to their potential, he says one cause is most prevalent. "The fundamental cause we found over and over again in some form or another was the fear of failure," he says. "Underachievers frequently think to themselves, 'If I try to go to the next level I could fall on my face, embarrass myself, or be exposed as not having the potential that everyone thinks I have.'"

Gault agrees, adding to the list a few more causes of under-achievement she commonly encounters, including procrasti-nation, the fear of success, and discouragement. "Another really important deterrent to success is having unresolved issues and conflicts clanking around in your head that keep you from taking decisive action," she says. "These burn up your time and energy, and until you're able to clear these out, you're going to be in a state of paralysis and not be able to act effectively." Mark Monro assesses the barriers to success more succinctly. As the onetime owner of a telecommunications firm who now runs FreshSuccess, a company specializing in fresh produce gift packages, Monro knows intimately the chal-lenges of building an effective career in sales.

"There are only two primary obstacles to success: other people and yourself," he says. "I don't know how many peo-ple have said to me, 'Why do you work so hard? Is it really worth it?' These negative rocks are hurled at me on a daily basis. That's when the self-doubt begins to grow, and you start asking, 'What am I doing?'"

SALES SUPPORT

Unquestionably, there are some unifying traits that nearly all successful people share, whether they're in business, sports, politics, or entertainment. To achieve success in sales, however, some characteristics are absolutely essential. Cliff Galyen heads up one of the top State Farm insurance agencies in the Southeast. He says that he realized early in his career that the level of his achievement was wholly dependent on his ability to help others.

"The first week I was in business, a woman I knew called me when she was going through a terrible divorce," he recalls. "I had coached her kids when they were in high school. She said, 'Cliff, you coached my children and now I need your help. Can you help me?' She needed car insurance, homeowner's insurance, health insurance, and life insurance. At that moment I realized that what I was doing was a big deal. It gave me the sense that I was helping people, that sales is not just about selling a product and making money. Whatever field you're in, sales has an objective, and in insurance it's to protect people— their health, their assets, and their homes.

"But when you focus strictly on the money part, you lose your sense of why you're here. You need to focus on the true aspect, and that is helping people overcome obstacles and problems they have. When you do that, the sales will come. I was able to see that early in my career, but many people aren't so lucky."

Monro agrees with Galyen, comparing the successful salesperson's role to that of a character in the blockbuster film, *Pay It Forward*. "Success in selling is often construed as simply the financial rewards, but I think it's seeing your product or service benefiting someone else," he explains. "You know that you didn't just sell someone better-priced pencils—you were able to help solve a specific problem. Maybe it was lowering the cost of customer acquisition, reducing churn, whatever— you know that you delivered tangible, measurable results. I think what we're doing in the selling process is a lot like the idea of 'paying it forward,' dedicating your effort, intelligence, and creativity to helping someone else. That's how I measure success in selling."

SOMETHING TO BELIEVE IN

During her years of study, Gault says, she has met and spoken with many people whom she felt had the potential to be top salespeople, but who nonetheless never succeeded. Invariably, she says, these people fell short because they lacked one of the critical core beliefs that provide the foundation of any success-ful life: "The first and possibly most important is to have a solid belief in yourself and your capabilities, to know that you have the power to influence the course of events," she says. "If at a gut level you believe that life is a crapshoot, and it's largely up to chance, and that what you do doesn't really make a whole lot of difference, you're not going to have the drive to get out there and make things happen or to sustain you when things go wrong."

Christian says that people who experience frequent ups and downs are most likely to lack this firm belief that they control their own destiny. "People who think that the locus of control is outside themselves operate differently and don't exploit all the opportunities that are out there," he says. "They'll be suc-cessful for a while and then go into a slump for a year and a half because they don't know how to identify what got them going in the wrong direction. Instead they attribute what's happening to the luck of the draw, and as a result they quit much sooner than somebody else who thinks, 'I've been through this before. I know what to do to bring things around again.' "

The second belief Gault mentions is the conviction that your actions and decisions matter, regardless of the outcome or the number of rejections you receive. "Maybe you won't always get the promotion or make the big sale; maybe your presentation will flop; your business may even go belly up," she says. "That's life. But success is not about how many failures we experience, but rather how fast we recover, learn from mistakes, and continue toward our goal. It's how we view failures and what we do about them that makes all the difference. You always need to pat yourself on the back for having the courage to take a risk, regardless of how it turns out."

Finally, people who hope to achieve success must hold the deep conviction that they are deserving of their desires and dreams. But, she cautions, this is not to be confused with arrogance or conceit.

"If at a deep, subconscious level you don't believe you deserve fame and fortune, or whatever the fruits of your labors may be, two consequences are likely," she argues. "One, you'll get right on the verge of achieving an important goal, and then you'll do something to sabotage it. I see that all the time. A second scenario is that you'll achieve some level of success, but it will be short-lived, and you won't be able to sustain it."

St. John agrees that believing in yourself is absolutely critical to long-term success, but he often disagrees with what many success theorists and motivational speakers consider the best way to firm up these beliefs. "Anyone who has been to a motivational seminar has heard that other people can't love you until you love yourself," he says. "So people wind up trying so hard to love themselves, but they just can't. But I believe it's the other way around—that you can't love yourself until other people love you.

"I compare it to Jimmy Stewart's character in *It's a Wonderful Life*. Because of an $8,000 life insurance policy, he believed he was more valuable dead than alive. Not until his guardian angel came down and showed him how many people's lives he touched did he understand his worth. He couldn't know it on his own, and that's the key. I feel that, to a degree, we're all like that. Introspection is important, but it will never let you know your own value. We can never know who we are except through the eyes of someone who loves us as we are. I bet there is not an example of a truly successful person who didn't have someone else in their life who believed in them when they couldn't believe in themselves."

SCORING GOALS

All theorizing aside, are there actual steps that people can take today to jump-start their drive to succeed, whether in the personal or professional arena? Absolutely, say the experts. Once you've cleared your head of unresolved conflicts and gotten in touch with a sense of purpose, Gault believes, you're ready to begin setting goals. But, she adds, once you've set a goal, act on it promptly. "This will establish an action pattern," she says. "Recognize that you're never going to be 100 percent ready for anything. We need to prepare ourselves as best we can and then act. You can correct as you go along."

St. John disagrees with the rush to set goals, however. In fact, he refers to the slavish dedication to goals and goal setting as one of the most pernicious directives emerging from today's success literature. "Of course, it sounds so logical that you have to set your goals," he says. "And let's be honest—humans are goal-oriented organisms. We will always go after something we want. Yet so many people feel trapped by the need to be always setting goals: 'The books tell me to set goals, so I guess I'd better do that.' What happens as a result is that they feel totally guilt-tripped if they ever stop to relax and breathe. That's why I believe people have to create goal-free zones. You've got to give yourself permission to stop. It sounds counterintuitive, but amazingly, we've also got to 'get it' that our worth doesn't come from our achievement."

INQUIRE WITHIN

Where Gault and St. John do agree, however, is on the importance of positive, effective self-talk. Both criticize what Gault calls the "mindless repetition of a bunch of affirmations." After using affirmations for years to little effect, St. John says, he realized that questions work much better at activating the mind than statements. As a result, he says, he came up with a new strategy he calls "afformations."

"When you repeat to yourself 'I am so rich' and write it down a hundred times, your brain is going to respond automatically by saying to you, 'Yeah, right. I don't feel so rich,' " St. John explains. "That's just what the brain does. It looks for reasons to dispute your statement. At the same time, if I ask you, 'Why is the sky blue?' your brain would immediately begin searching for the answer. You may not know, but you're searching. Realizing this, I asked myself, 'If that's how the brain works, why don't we cut out the middleman and go right to the end?' So instead of saying 'I am so rich' and having your brain refute you, why not ask the question, 'Why am I so rich?' When you put it this way the brain responds very differently—your brain assumes that you are rich and begins looking for reasons why."

In fact, St. John says, people use affirmations like these every day, but in a negative way. They ask themselves, "Why do I fail? Why don't I make enough money? Why can't I get ahead?" By simply turning these destructive questions into constructive afformations, he says, people will begin to believe their own positive thoughts much more easily. For example, he says, ask yourself the question, "Why am I such a great conversationalist?" Rather than stepping back to think about whether the question itself is legitimate, most people will instinctively begin thinking, "Well, I have a lot to say; I have a range of interests; I'm curious about other people . . ."

Ultimately, of course, it's up to individuals to determine what tactics and strategies work for them to help them build confidence and to continue working toward their own personal definitions of success. In sales, one of the biggest stumbling blocks is rejection. Ever upbeat, FreshSuccess's Monro says he has developed a mental exercise for dealing with the inevitable noes. "When someone says, 'I'm not interested' to me," he explains, "I think to myself, 'That's okay, your business isn't going to be as successful as it would have been if you'd implemented our program.' I'm going to find the next person or company where they understand the value of what I'm doing and where they'll say, 'Yeah, this is going to help us be successful.' "

Eric Anderson, a national sales manager with Power Merchandising Corporation in Delavan, Wisconsin, notes that success is often more likely to come when one seeks out other people who will exert a positive influence. "It's always been a goal of mine to surround myself with people who are better than I am," he says. "Even in high school I would hang out with the kids who were smarter, who had a little more on the ball. That's how I always felt I could elevate my surroundings. Then when I got into the work world, instead of hanging around the watercooler with the guys at my level, I tried to socialize with or be around the people at the next level up. I always wanted to be around people I could learn from."

In the same vein, Anderson says that mentors have played an important role in his success, helping him when necessary and giving him opportunities to prove himself. In today's environment, he believes that individuals intent on learning and growing must take the responsibility for seeking out mentors. "It's incumbent on the individual who wants that interaction to go out and find it," he explains. "That may not have been the case 15 years ago, but today people are a little more protective of themselves. But a mentor can do a great deal for you. A mentor can act as a sounding board, can offer perspectives you might not have considered yourself, or give ideas for a different approach to an issue. Plus, there are times when going to a manager might expose a weakness. You can go to your mentor first and say, 'I've got this problem. How do I approach it so I don't look like an idiot to my boss?' In the end, your boss doesn't know that you have a mentor, just that you handled a situation with maturity and professionalism."

Monro says he also uses other people to help inspire him to continue to work through any self-doubt that might well up. One particularly poignant and motivational individual he mentions is Christopher Reeve. "Here's a guy who was on top of the world and was then dealt a bad card," he says. "Responding to that bad card, he's not saying, 'Woe is me.' Instead, he said, 'You know what? It is what it is.' Thinking about his example, I feel like I need to stop for a second and say to myself, 'Enough with the BS about how difficult my life is and how I'm not making enough money. I'm alive, I can walk, I have all my physical abilities, so I need to get to work and stop bemoaning my petty troubles and how difficult life is.' "

JUST DO IT

For many people who are wallowing in a negative spiral or who have merely plateaued and are looking for a way to take the next step forward, these ideas will provide fodder for making positive change in their lives. But therein lies the key. As Gault points out, listening to tapes, reading, and thinking about doing things differently are not enough. The most critical step is to act.

"To permanently stamp these new beliefs in your mind, you do have to act on them," she says. "When we act as if something is so, it becomes so. Yes, you are going to meet resistance. It's just like when you start a new exercise program. The muscles are tight and stiff and they resist. The same is true with mental muscles. At first, if you've been running on self-defeating thoughts and beliefs, they're going to resist any new ideas. So you need to continually practice running the new beliefs in your mind at regular intervals and acting on them. There's a back-and-forth process between your beliefs and your actions. You can't just think your way to success."

LIFT YOUR SPIRITS

A former magician finds that increased motivation is no sleight of hand. When Michael Jeffreys presents motivational speeches to salespeople, he starts by borrowing a dollar bill from a member of the audience and, poof, turning it into a $100 bill. "That grabs their attention," says the former magician. "It's a visual reminder of why we're here."

While a magic trick may grab audience attention for an instant, the motivational message of superstars who make their living helping people incorporate a can-do attitude into daily life lingers long after the stage lights have dimmed. Jeffreys draws on his magic skills during speeches and motivates with attention-getting devices. Other top motivational speakers have their own methods, which Jeffreys studied in detail for his book *Success Secrets of the Motivational Superstars,* a compelling portrait of 15 top motivational speakers, including Mike Ferry, Anthony Robbins, and Danielle Kennedy.

Such speakers, who may earn anywhere from $5,000 to $125,000 for a two-hour stint, are dynamic individuals who have risen to stardom from humble origins. Many have overcome great obstacles in their quest for success and are willing to share their philosophies with others, especially salespeople who seek to emulate their winning ways. After studying the speakers, Jeffreys determined that while each has his or her own specialty, they share eight secret success traits. "If you integrate these ways of thinking into your own belief system, you will be able to succeed at anything you put your mind to," he says.

- **Success Secret 1:** Take 100 percent responsibility for your life. Instead of blaming your failures on others, look to yourself, because you are responsible for your own situation and must take the necessary action to change it.

Item: Abandoned by his parents at birth, Les Brown was labeled mentally retarded by his early teachers. But after being told in high school that "somebody else's opinion of you does not have to become your reality," his life changed. He went on to become an author, a state legislator, and a successful public speaker. By taking responsibility for his life, Brown became empowered, and you can, too, says Jeffreys.

- **Success Secret 2:** Stay focused. You must stay focused on your goal to achieve it, Jeffreys says, even if this means giving up some of the things you'd rather do. "Every day, ask yourself, 'Is what I'm doing right now bringing me closer to my goal?' If it's not, do something that will."

  Item: When suntan lotion tycoon Ron Rice quit his teaching and lifeguarding jobs to found Hawaiian Tropic, he felt he had to do everything himself. He mixed the lotion, bottled it, sold it, packed it into boxes, and delivered it to beaches and pool decks up and down the East Coast. He was relentless in his single-minded pursuit of his goal—to make Hawaiian Tropic a household name and himself a millionaire many times over. As he once told *Selling Power*, "In the early days all the other lifeguards used to kid me about how hard I was working and how little fun I was having. Now they're still working at the beach and I get to do whatever I want."

- **Success Secret 3:** Live your life on purpose. You must establish a purpose in life and live to fulfill it. You must love what you do, and when you do you'll be able to sway others. "You will find that people want to do business with you because they sense your commitment to giving your all," Jeffreys notes.

Item: After realizing that real estate agents needed help developing sales skills, motivator Mike Ferry founded The Mike Ferry Organization, a seminar and training company that now generates more than $10 million annually. Ferry discovered his purpose in life and has benefited greatly.

- **Success Secret 4:** Be willing to pay the price for your success. The idea here is to find out what it takes to succeed in your endeavor and do everything you have to do to achieve it.

    Item: Les Brown called more than 100 people a day to generate his first speaking gigs—and got a callus on his left ear as a result. "This callus is worth several million dollars," he says now.

- **Success Secret 5:** Become an expert in your field. Even if you already know how to sell, you could probably improve some of your skill sets. Everyone has room for improvement somewhere.

    Item: Even though she had already been named one of the 10 most electrifying speakers in North America, Patricia Fripp hired a private speech coach. Apparently, being one of the best wasn't good enough for Fripp, who sought to perfect her speaking skills. Salespeople should follow her lead and learn what it takes to be even better at their jobs.

- **Success Secret 6:** Write out a plan for achieving your goals. It's like having a map to get from one destination to another, Jeffreys says. Without the map you may get lost, and without a written plan you may lose touch with your goals in life.

Item: Tom Hopkins, who motivates and trains sales-people, not only wrote out his goals but even put a picture of one of them—a Lear jet—on his refrigerator. The jet was one of his 10-year goals.

- **Success Secret 7:** Never give up. It's amazing how many people are ready to throw in the towel at the least inconvenience or obstacle to success. In selling, studies have proven time and again that the salesperson who makes more calls often closes more sales.

    Item: Dr. Wayne Dyer spent a year on the road promoting a book he had written. His persistence paid off, because after making countless appearances at bookstores in small towns and on any radio or TV show that would have him, *Your Erroneous Zones* became the top-selling nonfiction book of the decade and Dr. Dyer appeared on *The Tonight Show.* "This is what the power of persistence can do for you," Jeffreys says.

- **Success Secret 8:** Don't delay. All of the motivational speakers studied by Jeffreys acted immediately to advance their careers, seizing every opportunity to move ahead. "The clock is ticking. There are no time-outs," Jeffreys notes. The time for success is now.

    Item: The day before Mary Kay Ash was to launch her cosmetics business, her husband, who was to be the CFO of the business, died suddenly. Everyone told her to fold her tent and get a job. She listened politely to her lawyer, accountant, and friends and then went right ahead with her plan. Mary Kay cosmetics has given thousands of women around the world the leg up they needed to provide financial and psychological security for themselves and their families. If Mary Kay had stalled, where would they be now?

CHAPTER 8

STOP WAITING FOR HAPPINESS

Four Ways to Pursue It

Y OU KNOW BETTER than to think buyers will just fall into your lap. You have to go after them and put some effort into winning them. The same rule applies to happiness, but some people think that being happy is an emotional phenomenon utterly beyond their control that comes and goes mysteriously or visits only those with fame and fortune. Nothing could be further from the truth. Happiness is largely a choice, and if you want it, you should be prepared to work for it. If you're ready to reach for the happiness you deserve, choose to be happy, then make it happen with these four steps.

1. *Enjoy life.* Learn to view small problems for what they are—small—and don't let them eat away at you. Laugh more often (especially at yourself) and look for humor

in every problem. Take your work seriously, but take time off for yourself and your family as well. With balance between your professional and personal life, you'll enjoy the best of both worlds. Even boring routines like driving to work can be fun if you pop in a favorite CD or an inspiring tape. At work, try to turn mundane tasks into games when you can. Compete with other salespeople, for example, to find out who can set the most appointments in a single day, or talk to your manager about injecting more fun and excitement into an otherwise boring weekly meeting.

2. *Be responsible for your happiness.* Loving others should bring you happiness, but you should also realize that you are complete and self-reliant as an individual—not one-half of a whole. Involve yourself in clubs or activities you enjoy, so you feel that you have your own life instead of simply participating in someone else's. Recognize your value and give yourself credit for your accomplishments. With career and personal goals to motivate you, you will feel that your life has greater purpose and will take satisfaction in striving to meet your objectives. Don't blame others for your failures and disappointments; instead, analyze your mistakes and plan how you can avoid repeating them. Before you can feel in control of your happiness, first take control of your life.

3. *Know why you're here.* The great novelist Leo Tolstoy had more than his share of hardship, but found a way to rise above his circumstances, writing, "I believe that life must and can be a constant joy, and the wise person is always joyful." For those times when you ask yourself why we are here, the answer is *to enjoy it all!* Instead of

viewing life as a series of tests or trials, learn to view it as a gift. You don't have to jump for joy when you get a speeding ticket, but most of us would have to admit that the things we worry about don't really matter much in the grand scheme of things. Realize that happiness doesn't come from material things, but from inside. Examine yourself to see if you are sabotaging your own efforts to be happy—and lighten up!

4. *Join the happy set.* Optimism is infectious, so if you can't seem to cure your blues yourself, try hanging out with a more positive crowd. Notice other people's reactions to crises and how they cope. Listen to the way they talk and interact with others. You might even question them about how they maintain an upbeat attitude. Make a list of the specific differences in their behavior and yours. You may find that their attitude rubs off on you. When you see that others can indeed be happy in spite of their troubles, you'll have more faith in your ability to do the same. Whatever you choose to think about, whatever information you choose to absorb will determine your attitude, and your attitude affects how much success you will have and how soon you will have it. For a brighter mood and a brighter tomorrow, get your brain in gear today, and make a conscious decision to raise your spirits.

CHAPTER 9

LIKE YOURSELF BETTER

❧————————❧

Seven Steps for Becoming Your Own Best Friend

1. *Don't compare yourself with other people.* You were designed to be yourself and nobody else. There is no "normal." There is no "average." If you rate yourself by other people's standards, opinions, and abilities you will always come up short. You are at your best when you are comfortable being yourself.

2. *Stay in line with your conscience and your own moral standards.* It is almost impossible to like yourself when you feel guilty. Guilt comes from doing things you personally believe to be wrong. So get in touch with your own values, and live by them.

3. *Forgive yourself.* When you have broken your own principles, forgive yourself completely. You're human. You make mistakes. Acknowledge you were wrong, correct

the wrong behavior, and learn from it. Then, once and for all, put it out of your mind. The past is gone.

4. *Separate personal worth from performance.* You are not your work. As Wayne Dyer said, "If you are what you do, then when you don't, you aren't." So build your self-worth on your infinite value as a magnificently designed, intricately crafted human person. Your ultimate value comes from being human. And you are a human being, not a "human doing."

5. *Accept compliments from other people.* Don't say, "Well, it was really nothing." Instead say, "Thank you very much." Receive compliments and allow them to build you up. Savor them.

6. *Give yourself compliments.* Mark Twain said, "When I can't get a compliment from anyone else, I pay one to myself."

7. *Use this affirmation: "I like myself."* Say it with feeling. Say it in your mind throughout the day. Say it out loud when you are alone. Say it 10,000 times over the next year. Soon you will fully feel it.

CHAPTER 10

INQUIRE WITHIN

⌁————⌁

When Indecision Stalls Your Quest for Success,
Look Inward for Answers

B ECAUSE FORWARD MOMENTUM is important to any success plan, the ability to make decisions and move on is critical. When looking around you fails to point you in the right direction, try looking at what's going on inside you. Your own beliefs, needs, experiences, and dreams will help you make the right choice. Let these suggestions give you easier access to your inner wisdom.

1. *Have faith in your abilities.* Making decisions is easier when you understand your options. Understanding your options starts with a belief in your ability to do and achieve anything you want. In other words, the more you feel you are capable of doing, the more options

you are likely to give yourself. Think about times in the past when you have done something you thought you couldn't. If you can't remember any, open a history book and review some of humankind's greatest achievements and inventions to remind yourself that anything is possible. Know your strengths and weaknesses; take a course or read a book to enhance your selling skill; and stop talking yourself out of reaching for the top because you are afraid you won't succeed.

2. *Be decisive.* To make progress you have to take action, and to take action you have to make decisions. Understand that making decisions always involves risk, so be willing to take a chance instead of waiting for a guarantee that your choice is the right one. Weigh the short- and long-term pros and cons of your options and consider how easily you can reverse or recover from a bad decision to help you decide what to do. Also, let the time you take to make a decision reflect its importance; if little is at stake, don't take forever to make up your mind. Remember that forward motion in the wrong direction is often better than no forward motion at all.

3. *Let your wants and needs be your guide.* When the decision primarily affects your own life, you should be the one calling the shots. Also, you may be more motivated to make your decision pay off if the choice is yours alone. Try to remember the last time you got really excited about something—a ski vacation to Colorado, a new car, a huge sporting event—and use the memory to remind you of the things that motivate and fulfill you most. If you incorporate those things into

your goals, you will know that you are working for something that really matters to you. Finally, you know your selling talents better than anyone, so you should know best how to make the most of them.

4. *Trust your instincts.* Especially when your instincts have a good track record, think twice before you act against them. You might not always be able to put your finger on why you feel good or bad about a decision, but it's a good idea to trust your intuition anyway. Before you go against your instincts, carefully consider your reasons and what you stand to lose. Ask the opinions of others familiar with your situation and qualified to give advice on what course of action they recommend.

5. *Clear your head.* To do your best decision making, you need to be able to think clearly and put things in perspective. Contemplating yesterday's problems or failures, for example, may prevent you from making decisions to ensure your progress tomorrow. Save important decision making for times when you aren't besieged by professional or personal problems. For many people, exercise, meditation, and getting close to nature have a relaxing and calming effect. Take time every day to engage in an activity that helps you put the day's pressures behind you.

6. *Let solutions reveal themselves gradually.* In many ways, your life is like a jigsaw puzzle that comes together piece by piece. Only after you start connecting several pieces do you get a glimpse of the big picture. Be willing to wait for success. Time often reveals options that were unavailable before. In the meantime, lay the groundwork for the next steps you are most likely to

INQUIRE WITHIN

Before you seek out the best sales trainer to suit your team's needs, experts recommend that you run a preliminary needs analysis on your own sales organization. Following are a few questions recommended by Kevin Davis, author of *Getting into Your Customer's Head,* for managers to consider before approaching outside vendors:

- Do we need advanced skills, beginning skills, or something in the middle?

- Do our people need to work on how to develop needs?

- Where in the sales cycle are we typically getting engaged?

- How are our customers' decisions typically made?

- What do our salespeople need to do to differentiate our offerings more effectively from the competition?

- How should we teach them to do that?

- Why are we losing business when we lose it?

- What specific solutions or steps could we take in the sales process to improve our chances of winning?

- What are our top reps doing right that our less successful reps are not managing as effectively?

take. Try reviewing where you have been, where you are, and when you are going to reassess the secrets of your success so far to determine what might help you maintain it. Also, remember that just because you are waiting to make a move in one area doesn't mean you can't continue your forward progress in other areas.

7. *Seek spiritual guidance.* When you can't figure out what to do from clues in this world, consider turning your attention out of this world. Instead of begging or pleading for a specific result, keep an open mind and simply ask for guidance from your Higher Power. If nothing else, praying or meditating may bring you the peace of mind that can help you make the right decision. Be patient waiting for your answer, and look for it in a variety of forms: an inner voice that urges you to take a particular course of action, a strong feeling, or a new and significant person entering your life.

8. *Be willing to implement the answer.* To move forward, you have to take that first step. When a solution presents itself, look before you leap, but if the coast is clear, go ahead and leap. If making big changes is intimidating for you, as it is for many people, analyze the solution you choose and identify what scares you about it—there's a good chance your fears are irrational, and identifying them will help you realize it. Make small changes one at a time if you prefer. You can also motivate yourself by remembering the costs of inaction (stagnation, stunted professional growth, frustration) and the benefits of action (progress, greater emotional and material rewards). Instead of letting fear limit your options, take courage, and you will have the freedom to go wherever your goals lead. Because we enjoy free

will, we also face choices, many of which have the potential to change our lives. The right choice may not always be crystal clear, but that doesn't mean it's inaccessible. Knowing what to do and which way to go is often simply a matter of knowing ourselves, so look inward to move onward.

CHAPTER 11

FOCUS ON THE POSITIVE

10 Rules for Success

1. Believe that you have already succeeded before you even begin the task. Act, dress, and speak, not for whom you are now but for whom you want to be.
2. Replace negative statements with positive phrases. Tell yourself "I am a good person." "I am a success." Practice this before going to bed and upon waking in the morning.
3. Take responsibility for your actions and your life. Never allow yourself to blame others for your lack of success. Even though an event might be caused by someone else and is out of your control, control your own reaction to the event.
4. Think positively about all of your accomplishments, no

matter how small they may appear to others. They are your building blocks of success.

5. Formulate a mission statement and keep it with you at all times.

6. Remind yourself of great success stories and the difficulties those people had in accomplishing their goals. Examples such as Helen Keller and Winston Churchill remind us that our problems and tribulations are small fish in a great sea.

7. When taking on a new project, ask yourself: "What is the worst that can happen?"

8. Allow yourself to make mistakes. It is an essential growth component.

9. Strive to be the best you can, not the best there is. You may find, however, that one leads to the other.

10. No one was born a great doctor, lawyer, or salesperson. We all came into the world as babies. We all become what we are based on the choices we make. You can choose success.

CHAPTER 12

LET MOTIVATION WORK MIRACLES

~~✷────────✷~~

Five Motivational Principles That Will
Get You over the Rough Spots

TO MOST OF US, motivation means getting revved up when we're bored, bouncing back when we're rejected, or getting psyched up for an important sales call. Motivation means life to Morris Goodman. He mastered the art of positive thinking to become a Top of the Table member as an estate planner and insurance salesman. Then on March 10, 1981, his motivational goals were from sales to survival when his private plane crashed, leaving him near death. Goodman shared his insights on motivation with thousands of people through his book *The Miracle Man,* which became a film by the same name from American Media. He is fully recovered—a fact that astounds the medical community—and wants to help others. Whether you're dealing with a physical tragedy like his or a sales problem, the following five motivational principles will get you over the rough spots and keep you moving toward a successful future.

1. *Positive thoughts breed positive action.* "Many times my doctors told me that I was being unrealistic to expect full recovery," recalls Goodman. "In fact, they said that maybe I'd eventually be able to sit in a wheelchair—unable to breath or eat without the aid of machines." But Goodman refused to be SNIOP'd (Susceptible to the Negative Influence of Other People). Instead, he constantly visualized himself as fully recovered. He communicated to everyone that he'd soon be back to his old self again. Morris's positive outlook generated the energy he needed to work on and accomplish his goals. If he had listened to the negative expectations of others, he might still be a vegetable.

2. *Be the first.* "My diaphragm was crushed in the accident, so everyone said I'd never breathe on my own—no one could breathe without a diaphragm," Goodman explains. "But I kept remembering how no one was supposed to be able to run a mile in less than four minutes—until Roger Bannister did it in 1954. Since then, lots of people have done it." Goodman practiced breathing in and out with his respirator until one day he started to breathe on his own. His stomach muscles took over the job of his irreparable diaphram. Morris was the first, and he hopes that others will follow. Just because something has never been done doesn't mean that it can't be done.

3. *Persistence pays off.* "Relearning how to walk was an incredibly painful process," says Goodman, as he remembers his atrophied muscles, sense of imbalance and feelings of defeat. "If I'd quit anywhere along the line, I'd still be in a bed, a wheelchair, or I'd need a walker or crutches. Because I promised myself I'd walk again, I kept at it—and it was worth it." Surrounded by signs like "No Pain, No Gain," Goodman never lost sight of his goal to walk on his own. Falls, pain, and frustration are now memories of the difficult path he took. But his persistence paid off, and today he walks around just as you and I do.

4. *Take one goal at a time.* Rather than tackle all of his problems, Goodman selected one at a time and committed himself to each one until it was achieved. As he reached each goal, his confidence soared, helping him through the next one. By breaking large, long-term goals into smaller, short-term tasks, you gain momentum and confidence that motivate you to continue on toward your ultimate goal. "Unless you have a plan, a goal to strive for, you end up going around in circles and you get nothing done," notes Goodman, who was deluged with major objectives like breathing, eating, speaking, and walking. "If I'd tried to accomplish everything at once, I'd still be working on most."

5. *What you give out you get back.* "The best motivation is not necessarily self-directed," Goodman says. "Often, helping other people feel good or motivating them to meet their goals gives a super boost to your own morale." During his stays in hospitals and rehabilita-

tion centers, Goodman shared his hope and his faith in people with the medical staff and fellow patients. Many of them say that he changed their outlook on life and expanded their belief in what is possible. Their positive feedback gives him the motivation to keep going. Whether it's your life or your career that's on the line, motivation can work miracles.

CHAPTER 13

SEEK OUT OPPORTUNITIES

❧———————❧

Proven Tips for Purpose-Driven Sales

THE MOTIVATION STRATEGIES in this chapter are based on an interview with Omar Periu, who has spent over a decade educating salespeople, leaders, and entrepreneurs worldwide. He has personally delivered 5,000 seminars, workshops, and training programs for 2 million people in more than two-thirds of the Fortune 500.

Motivation is choosing to do what you would rather not do. Motivated sales reps keep working on an opportunity until it successfully results in a sale. Unmotivated sales reps find multiple excuses for not doing things that would lead to a sale. Motivation is the great difference between successful sales reps and unsuccessful sales reps. Your ability to motivate yourself depends directly on your belief system. People who share the following three core beliefs find it easy to keep motivated:

1. *I am confident.* If you believe in yourself, you tend to see problems and challenges as speed bumps rather than as roadblocks. You possess certainty that you'll eventually succeed.
2. *I am committed.* If, in your heart of hearts, you are absolutely determined to succeed, you'll find that motivation emerges naturally from that commitment.
3. *I am in control.* If you view yourself as the captain of your destiny rather than as a pawn of fate, you'll have the motivation to continue moving forward—even when the going gets tough.

By contrast, there is a set of beliefs (unfortunately quite common) that thwart any attempt to become motivated. People who buy into the following three core beliefs find it terrifically difficult to get motivated:

1. *Nobody believes in me, so why try?* Some people define themselves based upon how they suspect their boss, coworkers, relatives, and friends see them. Convinced that people think poorly of them, such people suffer from low self-esteem and lack of confidence.
2. *I've failed before, so why try?* Some people believe that failure is so unpleasant that it must be avoided at all costs. They avoid any situations where failure is a risk. Because any meaningful endeavor entails risk, such people seldom, if ever, accomplish anything significant.
3. *Fate controls destiny, so why try?* Some people believe their status in life and potential as a human being are determined at birth or by the circumstances of their lives. Believing this allows them to deflect the blame

for their failure onto things over which they have no control, thereby lessening the pain of failure.

The two belief systems are directly opposed to each other. Most people are somewhere on a sliding scale between the two poles. To become motivated, you need to slide your own beliefs toward the pole that creates motivation rather than the pole that thwarts it.

HOW DO YOU GET MOTIVATED?

To reinforce the beliefs that will create motivation, you need to build a mental framework that supports motivating beliefs and makes the alternative beliefs sound silly and strange. Here is a seven-step program for creating that mental framework:

Step 1. *Find your purpose.* Why are you working? Why are you in sales? Only you can answer these questions. Some individuals are drawn to sales because they genuinely like helping people and would get bored if they weren't making money. Other individuals are simply working for a paycheck or to feed their families. No one purpose is inherently better than another. However, you need to know your purpose so that the prospect of fulfilling that purpose keeps you motivated.

Step 2. *Tie your purpose to your product.* Since you've identified why you're working and why you're in sales, the product (or service) that you're selling is the vehicle through which you can fulfill your purpose. The more closely you associate your purpose with the product you have to sell, the easier it will be to motivate yourself to do what's necessary to make a sale.

Step 3. *Tie your purpose to your manager's objectives.* In most cases, your manager wants you to be successful, because that helps him or her fulfill objectives. If you view your manager's objectives as being in line with your purpose, then those objectives can become a spur to your own success.

Step 4. *Tie your purpose to your company's strategy.* The reason you have a product or service to sell is that your company has created a product or service. Helping your firm fulfill its strategy not only helps you fulfill your purpose, but also helps your friends and colleagues fulfill theirs.

Step 5. *Create ambitious goals for yourself.* Now that you've got everything aligned, it's time to set ambitious goals that, if achieved, will create success for yourself, your products, your manager, and your company. Ideally, these goals should be greater than just making your quota. You need goals that will inspire you to achieve them.

Step 6. *Create a workable but flexible plan.* Create a step-by-step plan that constantly brings you closer to your goals, thereby building additional confidence, commitment, and the feeling that you're in control of your destiny. If you aren't sure how to build a plan that will work, get the help of somebody who's already achieved what you want to achieve.

Step 7. *Take massive action, starting now.* Success is now just a matter of executing your plan and adjusting it as necessary to achieve your goals. To start on the right foot, as soon as you write your plan, immediately take some action to achieve that plan. Motivation feeds on action. You want to build momentum that will continue to carry you toward your goal.

HOW DO YOU STAY MOTIVATED?

Since the world isn't perfect (alas!), you're going to run into challenges that might disappoint you. However, if you regularly practice the following four disciplines, you'll be able to transform those challenges into additional motivation. Condition your mind. If you're like most people, your mind sometimes drifts into negative thoughts. To keep this from happening, fill your mind with inspiring ideas and powerful examples of success that will reinforce your confidence and resolve. The most convenient way to do this is with motivational CDs, which can be played while you're on the road.

1. *Condition your body.* It takes physical energy to take massive action. If you're too tired to do more than the minimum, your chances for success are greatly reduced. Daily aerobic exercise is the best way to keep your body in condition to achieve your goals.
2. *Avoid negative people.* Social pressure is one of the most powerful psychological forces in the world. If the people around you are unmotivated, you'll be fighting an uphill battle to stay motivated. Treat people with negative thought patterns as if they are mentally ill. (That's not far from the truth, by the way.) Don't take anything they say seriously.
3. *Remain flexible.* No plan should be cast in concrete. You made the plan, so you can change it to make it lead more quickly to your goals. Achieving a goal is like

walking to a destination that you can see in the distance. As you get closer, you'll see things that were outside of your vision at the start. Change your plan so that it matches your new perception of circumstances. With regular practice, these disciplines will eventually become habitual. As you practice them, you'll not only notice a rapid increase in your own level of motivation, but also you'll find that, over time, motivation becomes an ingrained element of your basic personality. To summarize, here's how to keep motivated:

- Always act with a purpose.
- Take responsibility for your own results.
- Always stretch yourself past your limits on a daily basis.
- Don't wait for perfection; just do it now!
- Build an inspirational library for your office, home, and transportation.
- Be careful of what you eat, because it takes energy to succeed.
- Hang around with others who are motivated.

FOR SALES MANAGERS: KEEPING YOUR TEAM MOTIVATED

The following 12-step guide will help your sales team get motivated and stay motivated, thereby resulting in higher sales. This training session will take approximately 25 minutes.

1. Before the meeting, prepare a slide summarizing the contents of this article. (Or have your firm purchase a set of motivational CDs for everyone on your team.)

2. Open the meeting by explaining that the team is going to be working on motivation. Admit freely that you're not a motiva-

tional speaker and you're aware that, when it comes to motivation, there are limitations on what can be accomplished in the current setting.

3. Using the slide you've prepared, review the basic concepts of motivation, using (when appropriate) anecdotes from your own experience. On completion of this step, you should be about 10 minutes into the meeting.

4. Have your team take out writing materials. Explain that you're going to help them get in touch with some of the sources of their motivation. Make certain they realize they're not going to be put on the spot, and whatever they write down will be solely for their own benefit.

5. Ask them to write down the answer to the following question: What are three things you really appreciate—or could appreciate—about your ability to sell? Give them approximately three minutes to respond.

6. Now ask them, what are three things that are really great about our product (or service)? Give them approximately three minutes to respond.

7. Now ask them, what are three things that are really great about our company? Give them approximately three minutes to respond.

8. Now ask them, what are three things you really appreciate—or could appreciate—about your managers at this company? Give them approximately three minutes to respond.

9. Now ask them, what are three things you really appreciate—or could appreciate—about our customers? Give them approximately three minutes to respond.

10. Ask the team whether they feel more motivated than they did at the beginning of the exercise. Point out that nothing in life is perfect, but focusing on what's positive is more likely to make you successful than focusing on everything else.

11. If you purchased motivational CDs for the team, hand them out at this time and suggest that they listen to them when they're on the road.

12. Thank everyone for his or her participation. Let them know you appreciate them as employees, which is one of the ways you keep yourself motivated.

QUICK TIPS FOR YOUR NEXT SALES MEETING

Here are some thoughts and observations that can help your team stay motivated:

- Most people live lives of quiet desperation because they've never learned to manage their minds and emotions.
- Any question that begins with the phrase "What's wrong with [such and such or so and so] . . ." is wasted mental effort, because it assumes there's an insurmountable problem.
- Today's failure can breed tomorrow's success, provided you learn something valuable from the experience.
- Today's success can breed tomorrow's failure if you let success make you complacent about staying and keeping motivated.

- Goals that contain the phrase "I'll try . . ." don't work; if you want goals that motivate you, use powerful phrases such as "I will" or "I must."
- What holds most people back is fear of failure, but if you don't take action, you'll fail by default, so what have you got to lose?
- What you say reinforces what you think, so if something is about to come out of your mouth that doesn't serve your purpose, just keep quiet.

CHAPTER 14

DEVELOP A POSITIVE ATTITUDE

—⁓——⁓—

Four Methods for Keeping the Right Mindset

THE FOLLOWING MOTIVATIONAL TECHNIQUES are based on an interview with Jeff Keller, author of the best-selling book *Attitude Is Everything: Change Your Attitude . . . and You Change Your Life*. Using speeches, seminars, writing, audio programs, and video programs, Keller helps organizations develop achievers by providing specific techniques to foster a more positive, winning attitude.

Most sales professionals understand that a positive attitude—comprising optimism, expectancy, and enthusiasm—is a key element, perhaps *the* key element, of top sales performance. Despite knowing this, most sales professionals find it extraordinarily difficult to approach work with a positive attitude each and every day. This is because they wrongly believe that one's attitude is the result of exterior circumstances rather than something that is under their own control.

Attitude is not the result of what happens in the world but how one decides to interpret what happens in the world. Take the weather, for example. In the United States, many people feel depressed when it's raining and uplifted when it's sunny. In the Middle East, many people feel the exact opposite— a cooling rain is an excuse to have a picnic under a tree. Similarly, many adults grumble when it snows, while most children are delighted. This illustrates that one's attitude toward the weather is essentially arbitrary. It's not the weather but the interpretation of what the weather means that creates the attitude.

Arguing that children like snow because they don't have to go to school is missing the point. A snowbound child could just as easily mope around inside and complain about not being able to play croquet because it's snowing. Similarly, a sales rep making a sales call while it's snowing could grouse about the extra drive time or could look forward to the appreciation a customer might feel because that rep is committed enough to fight the weather to make the meeting.

In short, attitude is the mental filter through which one sees the world. Some see the world through a filter of optimism: no matter what happens they always make lemonade from the lemons. Every truly great sales professional thinks this way. Others see the world through a filter of pessimism: no matter what happens, they always find the cloud in the silver lining. People who think this way are usually terrible at sales.

Most sales reps, however, don't belong to either extreme. Instead, most sales reps (indeed, most people) have a variable filter that creates resourceful attitudes and nonresourceful ones based upon arbitrary interpretations of events. The challenge is to trade their variable and out-of-control mental filter for a consciously optimistic filter. This will consistently create the attitude that results in top sales performance. Four methods for accomplishing this feat follow.

METHOD 1: REDEFINE THE MEANING OF EXTERIOR EVENTS

Sales reps who have trouble maintaining a positive attitude are almost always letting arbitrary exterior events automatically trigger bad feelings. For example, a sales rep might become annoyed and defensive prior to a customer call simply by running into a series of red lights during the drive. To that sales rep, the red lights mean that it's an unlucky day. As a result, the sales rep walks into the customer meeting feeling depressed and defensive.

To get a different result, you must modify your interpretation of exterior events that formerly triggered your bad attitude. Once those events have a different meaning, they won't be able to trigger a bad attitude. For example, the sales rep in the example might see a series of red lights as an indication of how smart it was to leave early for the call. Or, if the sales rep is late because of the delays, the red lights can be an opportunity to collect thoughts and decide upon a damage-control strategy.

Many sales professionals view so-called failures (lost sales, missed calls, bad prospects) as triggers for bad attitude. However, it's also possible to view failures as learning experiences that point out the adjustments you must make in order to be more successful. Rather than becoming irritated by a failure, it makes more sense to consider that if you never fail, it means that you are taking no risks. Even the best sales rep doesn't close every sale. If you make it your business to learn from every setback and stay focused on your end result, failure simply becomes a way station on the road to success.

METHOD 2: START EACH DAY WITH AT LEAST 15 MINUTES OF POSITIVE INPUT

It's easier to achieve and maintain a positive attitude if you have a library of positive thoughts in your head. You can draw upon them if the day doesn't go exactly as you'd prefer. Starting each day reading, or listening, helps ensure that you have such a library to draw upon. Consider reading an inspirational book right after you wake up. You might also want to spend your commute time listening to motivational tapes rather than the news. Set a target of at least 15 minutes a day. If you commit more time than this, you'll get more benefits.

Along these lines, don't forget that music is a time-honored way to manage your moods and attitudes. Consider investing in CDs of music that you find motivating and energizing. Use music to pump yourself up right before your big meetings or to cool you down when things get challenging.

METHOD 3: REDUCE YOUR EXPOSURE TO BROADCAST NEWS MEDIA

Our mass-media culture bombards us with highly emotional messages that are intended to lead us to buy a particular product. Such mental manipulation is fairly obvious when it comes to television commercials (e.g., using sex to sell beer), but there are more subtle influences that can be highly toxic to your overall attitude about life. In particular, overexposure to the news media can be a real killer of a positive attitude. Thirty years ago, news programs primarily provided people with information intended to help them understand the issues of the day. Today, most news broadcasts consist of infotainment specifically crafted to support commercial messages. Much of today's news programming consists of "if-it-bleeds-it-leads" stories followed by commercials offering some form of security or comfort. The idea is to amp up your fear, anger, or frustration and then provide you with an action such as buying comfort food that promises to relieve the pressure.

This constant flow of negative imagery and commentary cannot only destroy a positive attitude, but it can also actively create a negative attitude about life and the world. Therefore, if you want to maintain a positive mood, you should consider reducing, or even eliminating, your exposure to broadcast news programming.

METHOD 4: AVOID PEOPLE WHO HAVE A CONTAGIOUS NEGATIVE ATTITUDE

Spending time with people who have a negative view of life makes it difficult for you to maintain a positive attitude. You probably have one or more friends, relatives, or acquaintances who make you feel tired and drained. They always seem to have something sour to say; criticisms come to their lips far more quickly than compliments. If you tell them of a success that you've had, their congratulations ring hollow. You sense that they'd just as soon see you fail. What a drag (literally)!

Such people are toxic to your attitude (and to your success in sales) because if they're not actively tearing down your enthusiasm, they're trying to make you think the same way they do about the world. If you want to maintain a positive attitude, you should consider sharply limiting your daily exposure to such people. Don't show up at the daily watercooler "complain-fest." Don't go to lunch with the grouse-and-grumble crowd. If you can't avoid these people, don't get drawn into lengthy gripe sessions. Limit your conversation to business issues you need to address and change the subject to a positive topic as soon as possible.

FOR SALES MANAGERS: QUICK TIPS FOR MOTIVATING YOUR SALES TEAM

If team members aren't getting the best results or have been discouraged by repeated failures, suggest that they ask themselves the following questions.

1. *Do I have an unrealistic timetable?* Success is usually achieved one step at a time. Be patient with yourself, and resist the temptation to compare your progress to that of others.

2. *Am I truly committed?* Be willing to do whatever it takes (within legal and ethical bounds, of course!) to banish any thought of giving up before you accomplish your objective.

3. *Do I have too many discouraging influences?* Surround yourself with people who support and believe in you. If you hang around with people who are highly critical or who are doing very little in their own lives, your energy and enthusiasm will be drained.

146

4. *Am I preparing to succeed?* Are you taking steps to learn everything you can about accomplishing your goal? Are you reading books, listening to tapes, taking courses, and networking with highly successful people in your field? Do you need a mentor or a coach?

5. *Am I truly willing to fail?* In most cases, you will encounter setbacks before you finally succeed. When you are not afraid to fail, you're well on the way to success. View failure as an unavoidable yet vital component in your quest.

CHAPTER 15

SALES MANAGER'S TRAINING GUIDE

—❦———❦—

12 Steps to Improve Your Team's Ability to Cultivate
a Positive Attitude That Will Result in Better Sales

FOLLOWING ARE 12 PRACTICAL STEPS to improve your team's ability to cultivate a positive attitude that will result in better sales. This sales meeting should take about 20 minutes.

1. One month before this training session, make a commitment—and keep it—to follow the four methods described in Chapter 14. Maintain a positive attitude for most of the month. This is important, because unless you're a positive role model, any attempt on your part to encourage a positive attitude in your sales team will probably fail.

2. Explain to the team that the meeting is going to be about attitude. Tell them that there won't be any grad-

ing of performance and that the exercise is entirely for their own private benefit. However, suggest that they take this information seriously, because it will be important to their long-term success in sales.

3. Spend five minutes explaining the basic principles of attitude and how important it is to sales success. Illustrate this point with anecdotes from your own experiences and observations.

4. Have the team take out writing materials. Ask them to rate their attitude on a scale of 1 to 10 (1 being extremely negative and 10 being extremely positive). They should base their score on how the majority of the people in their life would rate them. Then ask the team members to estimate where their level of attitude would have to be in order for them to become top sales performers.

5. Explain how most people use events to trigger a poor attitude and how it's possible to redefine the meaning of events. Have each team member write down a daily event that tends to trigger a bad attitude. Then have them write a new meaning for (or new interpretation of) that event that will not trigger the bad attitude. Offer to help anyone who has problems with this step.

6. Have the team members list all the mass media they hear and see during a typical day. (This should include television programs, radio shows, newspapers, magazines, training materials, motivational tapes, etc.)

7. After they complete this, have them imagine that they've just experienced each of these media. Have them put an up arrow beside media experiences that make them feel positive, a down arrow next to experiences that

make them feel negative, and a straight arrow next to neutral experiences.

8. Ask the team members to estimate how much (on a scale of 1 to 10) their attitude would change if they eliminated negative media inputs.

9. Have the team members list 10 friends and colleagues with whom they spend time every week. Have them imagine that they've spent time with each of these people. Have them mark an arrow (up, down, or straight) next to each person's name, depending on the impact that person has on the team member's attitude.

10. Ask the team members to estimate how much (on a scale of 1 to 10) their attitude would change if they spent half as much time with the people who earned a down arrow and twice as much time with the people who earned an up arrow.

11. Explain how following the four methods to achieving a better attitude has positively influenced your own life over the past month. Point out that everyone is different, and everyone must make his or her own decisions about how much or how little time to spend on maintaining a positive attitude.

12. Reassure the team that they're not going to be judged on how they maintain a positive attitude, but suggest that they take active steps to follow the four methods. Then close the meeting.

PART 3

MOTIVATIONAL HEROES

*35 True Stories of Challenge
and Achievement*

#1

No Reason Not to Succeed

Erik Weihenmayer is one of the best rock climbers in the United States. He can scale vertical cliffs of rock or ice, and he has now climbed the highest peak on all seven continents. He stays in shape for climbing by running marathons and jogging up and downs stairs with a 70-pound backpack. He's also blind, but quickly brushes aside any talk of that being a handicap. "Blindness is a nuisance," he says, "but it's not the reason you can't do something."

Born with retinoschisis, a rare degenerative condition, Weihenmayer was totally blind by the age of 13. But he refused even at that age to let it stop him. Each time he fell or failed in his efforts to accomplish something, he picked himself up and attacked it from a different angle. The result is that today he can outperform many climbers blessed with 20/20 vision. "When I start something, I know I'm going to flop on my face. But failure is a real valid way of learning about something," he observes.

#2

Noble Strides

For years Maria Goeppert Mayer, a brilliant scientist, lived in the shadow of her husband, another brilliant scientist. He was her partner and supporter, but still she couldn't get a paying job, because at the time women were expected to be house-wives and mothers. Mayer persevered, working side by side with her husband and raising two children while doing land-mark scientific research.

In 1963, Mayer won the Nobel Prize in Physics for her groundbreaking work in models of the nucleus of atoms. Ironically, she received her first paid position shortly before winning. Mayer was only the second U.S. woman ever to win a Nobel prize and the first to do so in physics. Against all odds, Mayer worked, ignoring stereotypes and doing what she loved and believed in, until her accomplishments were recognized and rewarded.

#3

By the Rules

Born of Jamaican immigrant parents in Harlem, New York, Colin Powell was an unlikely candidate to become a national hero. He grew up in a multiethnic section of the South Bronx, then attended City College of New York. While in college Powell made the decision that would shape his life. He joined ROTC, quickly rising through the ranks to become commander of the unit. His career in the army was a series of successes sandwiched between two grueling tours in Vietnam and a mas-terful command of the Allied Forces in the Persian Gulf. Yet one of his most noteworthy achievements took place off the battlefield, as he overcame racial barriers to become the most powerful and respected officer in the military and eventually the U.S. Secretary of State. Throughout his career, Powell has lived by several rules: Get mad, then get over it; check small things; share credit; remain calm and be kind; have a vision and be demanding; and perpetual optimism is a force multiplier.

#4

How Sweet It Is

Ben Cohen and Jerry Greenfield could easily take the money and run. As the multimillionaire makers of Ben & Jerry's Homemade Ice Cream, it would be simple to keep making ice cream and pocketing money. But these two entrepreneurs, who launched their company in 1978 in a renovated gas station, believe corporations have a larger responsibility. Their aim, they say, is to "operate the company in a way that actively recognizes the central role that business plays in the structure of society by initiating innovative ways to improve the quality of life of a broad community—local, national, and international."

To meet that goal, Ben and Jerry give away 7.5 percent of their pretax earnings to "projects that exhibit creative problem solving and hopefulness." To channel the money in the best directions, the dairy duo created Ben & Jerry's Foundation, an organization managed by a nine-member employee board that considers proposals relating to children and families, disadvantaged groups, and the environment. The two CEOs also make helping the world fun and creative. When they launched their S'Mores ice cream bar, Ben and Jerry asked customers to petition Merriam-Webster to include the word "s'mores" in its next edition. Then they joined forces with the publisher to aid in the fight against illiteracy, donating dictionaries to every Literacy Volunteers of America affiliate in the country.

#5

Doctors without Borders

Many said it couldn't be done. But in 1971, a group of French doctors founded Medecins Sans Frontieres (MSF), the first nonmilitary, nongovernmental organization to offer emergency medical assistance. Many of the founders had worked for the Red Cross in Biafra. While they believed in the mission of the Red Cross, they also believed that there was too little medical assistance and too many administrative obstacles. So they set out on their own. Since then, MSF has helped victims in Honduras, Somalia, Burundi, Kosovo, and more than 80 other countries throughout the world.

With a stated MSF mission to assist those who have fallen victim to natural or human-made disasters and to bring attention to the many places most people have never heard of, MSF helps refurbish hospitals, staff vaccine programs, and initiate water and sanitation projects. The organization also works with local personnel in remote health care centers and poverty-stricken areas to bring health care up to acceptable levels. In 1999 MSF won the Nobel Prize for Peace.

#6

Humor from Ashes

"When I look back on my childhood I wonder how I survived at all. It was, of course, a miserable childhood: the happy childhood is hardly worth your while. Worse than the ordinary miserable childhood is the miserable Irish childhood and worse yet is the miserable Irish Catholic childhood." This is an excerpt from *Angela's Ashes,* by Frank McCourt, who had no idea that his memoir of growing up dreadfully poor in Ireland would touch so many people. The novelist's first book (*Angela's Ashes: A Memoir,* Touchstone Books, 1999) recounts his life growing up, starved for food and affection, with an alcoholic father and a mother who struggled to keep the family together.

In McCourt's young life, he encountered death, alcoholism, disease, humiliation, and misery beyond our worst nightmares. Yet he managed to turn it all around after returning to America (his birthplace) and writing about his childhood hardships, with humor and great insight, from a child's point of view. McCourt, who now lives in New York City, has written a second best-selling book, *'Tis* (Scribner).

McCourt's sense of humor helped him live through and survive the memory of terrible times. After all, what is humor but a positive spin on a negative world?

#7

Douglas MacArthur

Douglas MacArthur had a lot to live up to. His father had been a Union army hero during the Civil War and was awarded the Congressional Medal of Honor for his bravery. MacArthur's mother was ambitious for her son to be equally successful. In the face of so much pressure, the younger MacArthur shone. He graduated from West Point in 1903, and rose steadily in rank in the army. In World War I, he commanded a combat brigade in France and, despite being wounded three times, pressed forward with his troops, earning a reputation for bravery. He remained in the army until 1951. Not only was MacArthur one of the greatest generals in U.S. history, he and his father are the only father and son to both win the Congressional Medal of Honor.

#8

Amedeo Obici

When a ship carrying 11-year-old Amedeo Obici arrived from Italy at Bush Terminal in Brooklyn, New York, in 1887, the boy was ecstatic. His widowed mother had shown him letters from his uncle in America ever since young Amedeo could read, and getting there from his home in Oderzo, Italy, had become Obici's dream. Although he couldn't yet speak English, the Italian immigrant quickly found work as a bellhop and later as a fruit stand vendor in Scranton, Pennsylvania.

Obici was a hard worker, but he was also an innovator. In Pennsylvania, he invested in a peanut roaster, selling roasted peanuts first at his own fruit stand, then as a traveling salesman using a horse and wagon. Eventually, he developed his own method of blanching whole roasted peanuts and disposing of the shells, hiring six employees to work at his two large roasters.

Obici lived by one important rule in the early days of his business: Profits are not as important as repeat business. Rather than chase dollars, Obici concentrated on producing a quality product that his customers would want again and again. The money he did manage to put aside helped his friends, brought his family over from Italy, and, in his later years, endowed a hospital in memory of his wife. In his start-up days, Obici understood that his reputation, and ultimately the future of his company, would depend on the success of his product. It worked. Today the company Obici founded in partnership with Mario Peruzzi in 1906 is still an American icon. First called Planters Nut and Chocolate Company, the name has since been shortened to simply Planters.

#9

Amelia Earhardt

Best known today for her mysterious disappearance while attempting to circumnavigate the globe at the equator in her Lockheed Electra, Amelia Earhardt first earned her wings on a solo flight across the Atlantic. On that trip, she flew through a lightning storm and at one point almost crashed into the ocean. Nearing land, her damaged plane began to leak fuel, and Earhardt was forced to make an emergency landing in an Irish cow pasture. But she had made it, setting a new speed record (13 hours, 30 minutes) and becoming the first woman to cross the Atlantic alone.

#10

Bob Thompson

Bob Thompson believes that taking care of and rewarding employees is the most important part of running a business. Thompson began his own asphalt company in Detroit, Michigan, with $3,500 his wife had earned substitute teaching. He worked hard, sweated alongside his employees, and didn't collect a salary for five years. He set tough standards—road crews worked six days a week between the last frost of winter and the first frost of fall—but was always willing to roll up his sleeves and help out. That combination earned him the loyalty of his workers and enabled him to build the company into Michigan's largest asphalt and paving business.

When Thompson sold the company in July 1999 for $422 million, he decided to give something back to the laborers who had sweated for him over the years. He wrote checks totaling $128 million to his 550 employees. Checks were based on years of service, and 90 people went home millionaires. Thompson was notably absent when the checks were handed out, predicting the swell of emotions that would course through the company and preferring to remain clear of it. Indeed, many of the workers, to whom the checks were a complete surprise, broke down in tears. Thompson simply observed that it was "the right thing to do" and said he hoped his employees would remember him.

#11

The Great Payoff

The life story of Andrew Carnegie proves beyond any doubt that hard work pays. Still called "the richest man in the world" years after his death, Carnegie was born in Scotland, the son of a weaver. He crossed the Atlantic with his family in the mid-1800s and promptly began working as a bobbin boy in a cotton mill. After that, he worked at Western Union and the Pennsylvania Railroad before starting his own company, the Carnegie Steel Company, in Pittsburgh. After selling it to J.P. Morgan for $400 million at age 65, Carnegie began giving away his money—more than $350 million to philanthropic activities before his death. Carnegie expected others to do the same and was among the first to publicly advocate social responsibility for the rich.

#12

Dolly Good

On a shopping trip for her young nieces in the late 1980s, Pleasant T. Rowland decided she didn't care much for Barbie—or any other doll on the market at the time, for that matter.

"Here I was, in a generation of women at the forefront of redefining women's roles, and yet our daughters were playing with dolls that celebrated being a teen queen or a mommy," she said in *Fortune* magazine.

During a trip to historic Williamsburg, Virginia, Rowland was inspired to develop dolls that would evoke a sense of history and encourage girls to embrace the wholesome side of girlhood. In one weekend, she created three dolls—lifted straight from the pages of American history—complete with personalities and backstories.

Rowland had no formal business training or experience making dolls, so she used as a model an 18-inch doll she found in a storeroom at her employer Marshall Field's. (Nobody had paid any attention to this doll because it had crossed eyes.) Investing $1 million of her own savings from previous jobs, Rowland planned to sell her American Girls Collection through direct mail in her own catalog. Although friends who worked at catalog retail giant Lands' End thought her product line would never work (and told her so), Rowland's friends schooled her in the business of direct mail.

Rowland hired a marketing manager, who explained the concept to a focus group of mothers. They hated the idea. But when the manager trotted out a sample doll with her little bed, clothes, and accessories, the mothers changed their minds.

"The experience crystallized a very important lesson for me," Rowland said. "Success isn't in the concept. It's in the execution."

Still, many predicted ruin for Rowland. Convinced that most girls abandon dolls by about age 10, the toy industry ridiculed her for targeting the 8 to 12 age group. Rowland's own list-management company warned her not to mail more than 100,000 catalogs for her first round of orders. Putting her faith in her idea and the Christmas market, however, Rowland insisted on sending 500,000.

Three months after her first catalog came out, everyone was singing a different song. Rowland's impossible idea had earned $1.7 million in sales. Competitors, realizing that Rowland had hit market magic (now widely recognized as *tweens*), scrambled to catch up.

In her second year of business, Rowland's sales hit $7.6 million. In 1998, she opened her first American Girl store in Chicago, which featured a doll hospital, hair salon, live theater, and tearoom. It quickly became the top-selling retail store on Chicago's biggest shopping street. That same year, Rowland sold her company to Mattel for $700 million.

The American Girl empire currently boasts *American Girl* magazine (650,000 subscribers strong), a second American Girl store in New York City (a third will open in Los Angeles in 2006), *The American Girls Revue* (an original musical, starring girls, for girls) and American Girl books. To date, consumers have purchased more than 11 million American Girl dolls. The catalog, ranked among the top 25 in the country in sales, now offers eight different American Girl dolls and includes spin-off lines Bitty Baby and Angelina Ballerina.

At around $100 each, American Girl dolls aren't cheap, but, then, neither are girlhood memories. "We give girls chocolate cake with vitamins," Rowland told *Fortune*, adding that her products allow girls to be girls for a bit longer.

#13

Against the Odds

Unless you live in Indianapolis, Indiana, you may not know that starting out with $1.50 in 1905 an African American woman named C.J. Walker became America's first woman self-made millionaire. Walker opened the Madam C. J. Walker Manufacturing Company, the nation's first successful black-hair-care products firm, in Indianapolis. Her factory employed 50 people and she trained thousands of women at her beauty school. Walker also put together a 20,000-agent sales force throughout the United States, the Caribbean, and Central America. At a time when all odds were against women and African Americans in business, Walker broke all the rules and wound up a millionaire. Today, she is the only African American woman in the U.S. National Business Hall of Fame.

#14

Reach the Highest Goal

Don't tell Mark Wellman he can't climb mountains. Wellman, a former Yosemite park ranger, became the first paraplegic to climb the 3,200-foot face of El Capitan in 1989. It took Wellman seven days and four hours—an estimated 7,000 pull-ups—to reach the top. Wellman had been paralyzed from the waist down when he fell 100 feet while climbing in 1982. Wellman and his climbing partner, Mike Corbett, climbed Half Dome, another Yosemite challenge, in 1991. Wellman continues to inspire the world with his determination and willingness to challenge adversity by skiing, climbing, and touring. In 1993, Wellman skied 50 miles, becoming the first paraplegic to sit-ski unassisted across the Sierra Nevada Mountain Range, using only his arms. In July 1999, Wellman repeated the El Capitan ascent.

#15

Flights of Fancy

Birth out of wedlock was a lifelong curse in Europe during the early 1800s. John James Audubon thus went to great pains to hide the fact that he was the son of a French naval captain and an unmarried young French girl who worked for Captain Audubon on his sugar plantation in Haiti. John gave different people different stories about his birth and felt hopelessly defined by his illegitimacy. His hopelessness in business made things even worse. As a teenager, Audubon was sent to manage his father's plantation near Philadelphia, but had great difficulty grasping the details necessary to make the plantation flourish. Frustrated by the embarrassing circumstances of his birth, and now by his inability to run the plantation, Audubon viewed himself as a failure.

Then he met Lucy, the woman who would become his wife. Lucy remained steadfastly supportive of her husband throughout their early married years, as Audubon continued to struggle in business endeavors. However, Audubon began to devote more time to his true passion—drawing. A trip to England turned things around. There, people appreciated his work and made possible the publication of the 435 prints he had made between 1826 and 1838. In the 1830s Audubon wrote his *Ornithological Biography,* describing the habits of the birds in his drawings. This publication is now considered a masterpiece, as are many of his prints. When *Field & Stream* editor George Grinnell decided to form a bird preservation society in 1886, he knew exactly what it would be called—the Audubon Society, after the now-renowned naturalist and painter.

#16

Born Out of Adversity

Lee Iacocca was fired from Ford Motor Company in July 1978. The son of Italian immigrants had been president of the company for eight years, had been a Ford employee for 32 years, and had never worked anywhere else. Now he was out of a job. To make matters worse, Ford had agreed to provide Iacocca with an office until he found new work, but that office turned out to be an out-of-the-way room in an out-of-the-way warehouse with a small desk and a telephone.

It was Iacocca's greatest humiliation. Just the day before, he had been working in the office of the president with its own bathroom and adjacent living quarters. He'd had a staff of waiters at his call and a secretary to bring in filtered coffee in a mug. Now, all he had was a plastic coffee cup and a machine down the hall. It was a pivotal moment for Iacocca. He realized no one would help him but himself. "There are times in everyone's life when something constructive is born out of adversity," he wrote in his autobiography. "There are times when things seem so bad that you've got to grab your fate by the shoulders and shake it. I'm convinced it was that morning at the warehouse that pushed me to take on the presidency of Chrysler only a couple of weeks later."

Iacocca went on to become a legendary businessman who brought Chrysler back from bankruptcy through brilliant management tactics—all because he decided when he hit the bottom that no one would keep him there.

#17

Luck of the Drew

Although actor and comedian Drew Carey now gets the last laugh, there was nothing funny about his life before stardom. Carey was only eight when his father died, and a year later he was molested. As a college student at Kent State, he attempted suicide one night at a fraternity party. He returned to school but earned such poor grades that after five years he left without a degree. After drifting across the country and attempting suicide again, he began reading Wayne Dyer's *Your Erroneous Zones* and Og Mandino's *University of Success*—volumes he says helped turn him around. When a friend asked him to write some jokes for a radio show, Carey submitted material, and within months he took the stage at a comedy club. He made two appearances on *Star Search* in 1988, and in 1991 he appeared on *The Tonight Show*, after which his success snowballed. No matter how far you sink into the depths of despair, Carey proves you can always pull yourself up again.

#18

A Laughing Matter

After his father, Percy, lost his job, Jim Carrey and his entire family went to work in an Ontario factory. Jim and his siblings attended school by day, and then worked as security guards, assembly-line workers and janitors by night. Once an A student, Carrey's grades fell and he dropped out of school at age 16. Years later, before his phenomenal acting success, he made out a check to himself for $10 million for "acting services rendered," postdated it Thanksgiving Day 1995, and stuck it in his wallet as a reminder of his dream. Several days after Jim found out he would earn $10 million for a sequel to the hit movie *The Mask*, Percy Carrey died, and Jim put the check in his father's casket. Having proven that adversity is no deterrent to success, Carrey now ranks among Hollywood's most bankable actors.

#19

Shoot for the Moon

Smith College president Ruth Simmons ranks among the academic stars. With 11 brothers and sisters and parents who barely made a living raising cotton as tenant farmers, Ruth J. Simmons got acquainted with poverty at an early age. In school, classmates teased her for having only two different outfits to wear. She earned her teachers' attention for all the right reasons, however, and maintained an A average in high school. She earned a scholarship to Dillard University in New Orleans and graduated summa cum laude in 1967. Her outstanding performance in school proved a harbinger of even greater things to come. When on July 1, 1995, she was named president of Smith, a women's liberal-arts college in Massachusetts, Simmons became the first African American woman to hold that position at a top-ranked American college or university. From a poor background, but rich in spirit and determination, Simmons earned her place at the top.

#20

In It to Win It

In 1983, when Martina Navratilova was ranked the top women's tennis player in the world, she faced Kathy Horvath, ranked number 45, in a match. Navratilova had not lost a match that year and had lost only three times the year before, to highly ranked players. Horvath seemed to have no chance of defeating her opponent, but nonetheless won the first set 6 to 4. Navratilova took revenge in the second set, trouncing Horvath 6 to 0. Instead of coming unglued, though, Horvath poured it on and won the final set and match. She explained her victory by saying, "I was playing to win." Sometimes the will to win is stronger than any opponent.

#21

Come Out Swinging

At the 1998 U.S. Open in Kohler, Wisconsin, 20-year-old golf phenom and LPGA champion Se Ri Pak faced Jenny Chuasiriporn in the first 20-hole playoff in U.S. Open history. At the eighteenth hole, Pak's ball landed in a clump of grass inches from a body of water. Forced to take a drop and a penalty or to hit the ball from the hazard, Pak took off her shoes, stepped in the water, and with the ball sitting in the grass above her knees, knocked it out of the hazard. She missed par by a stroke on that hole, but the effort proved sufficient to tie her with Chuasiriporn. Pak won the resulting two-hole, sudden-death playoff with an 18-foot putt on the second hole. Despite the tremendous strain of head-to-head competition, Pak refused to crack under pressure and coolly met each challenge as it came, to win her second consecutive major title.

#22

Stoked for Success

Wendy Stoeker is living proof that you don't need wings to fly. As a freshman at the University of Florida, she took third place in the girls' state diving championship and was a member of the school's very competitive swim team. Her achievements go from admirable to unbelievable when you learn that she was born without arms. Instead of using her disadvantages as an excuse to fail, Wendy refuses to be limited by them. With determination and a positive attitude, nothing can stand in the way of your success, either.

#23

Make Your Own Miracle

After one side of his face suddenly became paralyzed at a Christmas party in 1986, writer Gregory White Smith found out that the benign brain tumor doctors had discovered 10 years earlier had suddenly turned malignant. Doctors told him he had just three to six months to live.

As he watched a weather report, Smith realized that just as weather forecasters could not guarantee their predictions, doctors couldn't guarantee a prognosis. He found a New York neuroradiologist, who used an experimental procedure to shrink the tumor by 50 percent, buying Smith the time he desperately needed. After five years, he found a surgeon capable of operating on tumors located in the same area of the brain as his. The surgeon removed much of the remaining tumor, and Smith now takes synthetic hormones to help stunt its growth. Even when the outlook was bleak, Smith recognized the difference between probability and certainty, refusing to give up and proving that when you fight the odds, you're that much closer to beating them.

#24

Decathlete's Feat

After decathlete Dan O'Brien lost his scholarship to the University of Idaho at Moscow due to years of partying and poor grades, he kept the electronic card giving him access to a dorm and the cafeteria until campus police threw him out with his belongings. In need of help, he turned to university track

172

coach Mike Keller and was readmitted to the school. After his last semester, O'Brien stayed in Moscow, training, delivering bottled water and rock salt to pay the rent, and nurturing a vision of holding the decathlon world record. Incredibly, he failed to make the team for the 1992 Olympics in Barcelona but persevered and, in September of that year, achieved his dream, breaking Daley Thompson's world record by beating his previous mark of 8,847 points. In 1996, O'Brien won a gold medal at the Atlanta Olympics and received one of the sports world's greatest honors: to appear on the front of the Wheaties box. Even when talent comes naturally, O'Brien's story shows you need discipline, effort, and persistence to make the most of it.

#25

Sears' Biggest Fan

For Sears chairman and CEO Edward A. Brennan, company loyalty knows no bounds. Brennan's grandfather had worked alongside founder Richard Sears, and two uncles were buyers for Sears. Brennan's father bought slacks for Sears, and as a child Brennan wore only dress slacks, even when playing baseball. Outside of school, the young Brennan sold newspapers, ironed shirts, and cooked meals for his father and brother and defended Sears with such zeal that his friends mocked him for it. Although at 15 Brennan took a job at Benson and Rixon, a men's clothing store, he started on the road to success at Sears in 1956, gradually working his way up, and 24 years later was named president and COO of the merchandising group. Whether you own it or not, your company's success can help to make or break your own. Cultivate loyalty to the business you work for and let it show in your efforts, and when business takes off, you, too, can enjoy the ride.

#26

Determined Dancer

So great was Wendy Whelan's desire to dance that nothing could stand in her way. At age 12 a pinched nerve revealed an overdeveloped muscle in her back and then scoliosis, a lateral curve of the spine inhibiting equal movement of both sides of the body. To correct the condition, that summer Whelan spent a month in traction. Out of bed, she wore a brace stretching from her neck to her pelvis, and still she danced, taking a class at the Louisville Ballet Academy in Kentucky. Unable to meet the demands of the entire class, Whelan did what she could—basic warm-up exercises and front and side extensions. Though she still wore the brace to school in the fall, she knew the gain would be worth the pain. In 1981, at age 14, her trials became triumph when she earned a scholarship for the summer program at the School of American Ballet in New York City, and she became a soloist with the New York City Ballet eight years later. The path to the top is seldom without suffering, but the ultimate rewards are usually well worth it.

#27

Best Actor

For Morgan Freeman, fate stepped in so he wouldn't miss his calling. Freeman's acting career began in the seventh grade with a part in a one-act play that won both the district and state championships in a statewide school theatrical competition. Freeman himself was named the best actor in the competition. After high school, Jackson State College in Jackson, Mississippi, offered Freeman a partial scholarship in theater, but Freeman chose to pursue his dream of becoming a fighter pilot instead. Despite scoring exceptionally well on the military exams, Freeman was assigned to be a radar mechanic, not a pilot. Fortunately, Freeman's loss also proved to be his gain. Only after being discharged in 1959 did he set out for Hollywood to embark on an acting career. For Freeman, one huge disappointment opened the door to even bigger success.

#28

A Truly Special Olympian

Born mentally retarded and legally blind, Loretta Claiborne endured a childhood that might have broken a child with less strength and parental support. Claiborne didn't walk until she was four years old and underwent operations on her eyes, a knee, and a foot. School brought little relief, as Claiborne was taunted cruelly by classmates who called her "Bozo the clown," "retard," and "simp." At age 12, Claiborne began running with her older brother, Hank, a high-school cross-country track athlete, and one night when he tossed her his towel after a workout and suggested that she use it, too, she realized that running might help her rise above her disabilities. She hasn't stopped running since, competing in the Boston Marathon in 1981 and finishing among the first 100 women to complete the race. She was named the Special Olympics Female Athlete of the Year in 1988 and won ESPN's Arthur Ashe Award for Courage in 1996. Claiborne had more reasons than most to feel sorry for herself, but chose to pursue success instead of wallowing in self-pity.

#29

Newsworthy

Broadcast journalist John Hockenberry hasn't been able to walk since a car accident left him paralyzed at age 19. To say he's been confined to a wheelchair, however, would be grossly inaccurate. On a job he took after the accident, a supervisor (who later became his wife) expressed doubt that he could fulfill his duties as an employment trainer in a nursing home for developmentally disabled adults. In response, Hockenberry got busy and brought his behind-schedule shift ahead of the game within his first week of work. After he uncharacteristically missed a deadline while reporting for National Public Radio in Oregon, Hockenberry called NPR in Washington to explain that he hadn't been able to get his wheelchair into a phone booth. The NPR staffers hadn't even known he had a disability. Later, on assignment in Amman, Jordan, Hockenberry pulled himself up four flights of stairs for an interview on the fourth floor of a building without an elevator. Instead of letting his physical abilities define his limits, Hockenberry decided for himself what he could and could not do and refused to let his wheelchair or anything else hold him back.

#30

Top of the (Trash) Heap

After getting his start in garbage, H. Wayne Huizenga climbed to the top of the heap. First, he spent three semesters in college (1957–1958) and a brief stint in the army, and then a family friend hired Huizenga to drive a garbage truck in Pompano Beach, Florida. In 1962, he tried to make a go of it in garbage on his own with one truck and $500 in accounts. After collecting trash from 2 a.m. until noon, Huizenga knocked on doors to sell new accounts. By the late 1960s, his truck fleet had grown from a single truck to 20 vehicles, and Huizenga was a millionaire. Expanding his interests, between 1987 and 1993 Huizenga built Blockbuster Video from a chain of 8 stores and 11 franchised establishments in Texas to more than 2,000 outlets nationwide. He was also the only person in the United States to own three professional sports clubs—the Miami Dolphins, the Florida Marlins, and the Florida Panthers. With a vision of what might be and the determination to make it happen, unglamorous beginnings can yield glorious success.

#31

Down but Not Out

On May 10, 1996, Dr. Beck Weathers, a pathologist from Dallas, Texas, was among a group of climbers on Everest caught unprepared when a sudden storm hit the mountain. Weathers and another climber were found in the ice and rock above 25,000 feet. Barely breathing, both climbers were left where they lay and reported dead.

Weathers's oxygen supply was gone. He had lost a mitten and couldn't zip his parka shut again. Hypothermia, delirium, and unconsciousness followed.

Then Weathers saw a vision of his family, and he knew he couldn't die. Hallucinating, the "dead" guy staggered into Camp IV the next day. No one expected him to live another night. His hands were frozen solid and his cheeks and nose were black with frostbite. Yet he refused to die.

Throughout his ordeal, Weathers maintained his optimism and good humor. In his book, *High Exposure,* climber David Breashears writes, "After all that death, after being judged dead himself not once but three times, this man's spirit was transcendent. He was a gift for all of us from that tragedy. Out of all that horror emerged this great spirit." Weathers's right hand was amputated; his left hand and face required extensive surgery. Ever philosophical, he observes, "If an ordinary person was able to survive these experiences and come out not just alive, but improved, so can anyone."

#32

Down-to-Earth Heroism: Cold Feet, Warm Heart

Snow lay on the ground on the cold December day in Milwaukee when 14-year-old Frank Daily boarded the number 10 bus after school. Soon after, the bus stopped for a very pregnant woman, who grasped the handrail, struggled aboard, and plopped into the seat behind the bus driver with her feet raised. But for a pair of torn stockings, her feet were bare. When the bus driver asked where her shoes were, she explained that after making sure her eight children had shoes, she had no money left to buy herself a pair. She'd gotten on the bus just to warm her feet, she said, and would ride around for a while if he didn't mind. Knowing she needed his shoes more than he did, Frank glanced down at his new Nike basketball sneakers, then pulled them off and handed them to the woman as he got off the bus. The driver called after him to ask his name and told Frank that in 20 years of bus driving he'd never seen anything to match what Frank had done.

Years later, Frank Daily went on to study Spanish and politics at Wake Forest University in Winston-Salem, North Carolina. He maintains that what he did that winter's day was no big deal and says, "We all have the potential to be heroic in some way." By fulfilling that potential, you stand to enrich your own life along with the lives of those you help.

#33

Supreme Success

For any law student who graduates first among the women in her class at Cornell University, then earns admission to Harvard Law School, edits the *Harvard Law Review,* and finishes Columbia Law School tied for first in her class, the doors of opportunity should open wide after graduation. For Ruth Bader Ginsburg, however, they slammed shut. When she graduated in 1959, discrimination was still alive and well in the law profession and elsewhere, and despite stellar academic achievements and impeccable credentials, Ginsburg was dismissed out of hand by one New York City law firm after another.

For Ginsburg, it was the latest in a series of discrimination-related obstacles. Years earlier, during her husband

Martin's military service at Fort Sill in Lawton, Oklahoma, she had applied at the local Social Security office for a position at the GS-5 level, only to be demoted to a GS-2 position after she revealed to supervisors that she was pregnant. Later, one of only nine women in her class at Harvard Law School, Ginsburg was questioned by the dean about how she and Martin could justify her taking up space when a man could be studying. Thankfully, many years earlier Ginsburg's mother, Celia, had ignited in her daughter a flame of ambition that such prejudice could not extinguish. Though Celia Bader died of cancer the day before her daughter's high school graduation, Ruth never forgot her mother's lessons on the value of discipline and hard work.

Ginsburg continued working tirelessly for opportunities that might have poured in for any man with her qualifications and finally earned a clerkship with federal district judge Edmund Palmieri. She finished her clerkship in 1961 and in 1963 became the second woman to join the faculty of Rutgers University Law School, one of only 20 women at the time to teach at a U.S. law school. Pregnant in 1965 with her second child, Ginsburg this time wore baggy clothes to hide her condition. She gave birth over the summer and returned to work in September, avoiding the disapproval she might have faced from colleagues.

Despite the opportunities she'd been denied because she was a woman, Jewish, and a mother, by the late 1960s Ginsburg had not yet recognized her enemy as discrimination. Then, the New Jersey affiliate of the American Civil Liberties Union began to refer sex discrimination cases to Ginsburg simply because sex discrimination was perceived as a women's issue—regardless of the client's gender. To prepare for the cases, Ginsburg took one month to read all of the available legal information on the subject.

With newfound awareness of discrimination and determination to fight it, in the early 1970s Ginsburg won several major victories for women and for herself. In her first important case, *Reed v. Reed,* Ginsburg helped convince the Supreme Court to overturn an Idaho law that gave precedence to men over women in naming the administrator of an estate. In 1972, Columbia Law School welcomed her as its first tenured female professor, and the next year she became general counsel to the ACLU.

Many of the cases Ginsburg tried in the 1970s continue to help discount gender-based stereotypes, including her final Supreme Court victory, *Duren v. Missouri,* in which she argued that Missouri laws making jury duty optional for women but mandatory for men reflected the state's view that women's citizenship was less valuable than men's. In 1980, President Carter nominated her to the United States Court of Appeals for the District of Columbia, in which position she wrote more than 300 opinions on significant issues from abortion to affirmative action.

In 1993, Ginsburg's nomination to the Supreme Court by President Clinton marked the crowning achievement of a lifetime of brilliant successes. She took the oath of office on August 10, and in her acceptance speech she thanked her mother, whom she called "the bravest and strongest person I have ever known." Celia Bader could hardly have wished for a greater legacy than a daughter who, despite the obstacles in her way, fulfilled her potential and then dedicated her life to helping to remove those obstacles so that women and other minorities everywhere might fulfill theirs.

#34

Imprint of Success

Although Katharine Graham grew up surrounded by the newspaper business, she was in her midforties before she began to learn anything about how it worked.

In 1933 Graham's father, Eugene Meyer, bought a small Washington, DC–based newspaper with a circulation of 50,000 at a bankruptcy sale for $825,000. Katharine was 16 years old.

However, Meyer's investment in the *Washington Post* was not a moneymaking proposition for many years. In 1935, he lost more than $1.3 million. By 1940, although circulation had increased to 130,000, the paper ran a deficit of $750,000—and even higher the next year. During World War II, the *Post* finally broke even.

True to her roots, after college Katharine Meyer worked as a reporter for the *San Francisco News*, later joining the staff of the *Post*. In 1940, she married Phil Graham. Lean, witty, charismatic, and hardworking, he had the right mix of physical, intellectual, and social charm. In addition to four children, she credited him with giving her life originality, irreverence for rules, and laughter. In 1946, Eugene Meyer named Phil Graham publisher of the paper. Two years later Meyer sold 5,000 shares of Class A common stock to his daughter and son-in-law at $48 per share.

As the years went by, Phil Graham drank heavily and suffered from manic depression. In 1963, he took his own life. In one instant, Katharine Graham lost both the husband she loved deeply and the CEO of their company. "Left alone," Graham stated, "no matter at what age or under what circumstance, you have to remake your life." In her Pulitzer Prize–winning autobiography *Personal History,* Graham describes her entrance into the business world as terrifying yet necessary. The board of the Washington Post Company elected her president, but she readily admitted she had no idea of the role she eventually would play.

One of Graham's greatest assets was her passionate devotion to the company and the newspaper. "I felt I had to make it work," she said. Also, she learned from her father and her husband that journalistic excellence must go hand in hand with profitability. In this area, she wisely surrounded herself with competent people, seeking their advice and counsel.

One of the most important people to influence her professional life was Warren Buffett. By September 1973, he had acquired around 410,000 shares of the company, and the next year he was elected to the board of directors. Graham recalled her first meeting with Buffett, who saw that she knew very little about business and finance. Furthermore, he sensed she was intimidated. Graham herself admitted she still felt uncomfortable and vulnerable with most issues regarding the business side of the company. But Buffett worked closely with her. "My business education began in earnest," Graham said. "He literally took me to business school, which was just what I needed."

Significant events in the early 1970s tested Graham's judgment and direction, giving her a measure of self-assurance. In 1971, the Pentagon Papers were first published in the *New York Times*. The Nixon White House asked the paper to suspend publication. Now the *Washington Post* had to decide whether or not to publish the infamous Pentagon Papers. Editorial said yes. Legal and advertising reminded Graham that the financial integrity of the paper was at stake. She came down on the side of the editors and "the obligation of a responsible newspaper."

The next year Graham and the *Post* gained greater notoriety with the paper's coverage of the Watergate break-in and the subsequent toppling of a president, and in 1975 the paper faced a long and ugly strike.

But Graham weathered all these storms with determination and diligence. She served as chairperson of the Washington Post Company's executive committee. She and her son Don, chairman and CEO, owned 60 percent of the company. In addition to the *Washington Post*, the Washington Post Company's holdings included *Newsweek*, half of the *International Herald Tribune* (Paris), more than 30 Maryland community newspapers, six television stations, and a regional sports cable network based in Detroit. In 1998, the company reported sales of $2.1 billion. By reshaping her life and pushing herself to exceed all expectations, Katharine Graham grew because of the adversity that might have crushed her spirit and ruined her chances for success.

#35

Famous Amos, the Muffin Man

In the early 1980s, the Famous Amos Cookie Company was booming. Its CEO, Wally Amos, was at last enjoying the fruits of his entrepreneurial labor. He had come a long way to head this $10 million a year company. The first 12 years of his life were spent "in the Colored section of Tallahassee,

Florida, not knowing much about what was beyond it," Amos writes in his book, *Watermelon Magic: Seeds of Wisdom, Slices of Life*. He spent the rest of his teen years suffering from low self-esteem in the multiracial, multiethnic schools of New York City. But he managed to put all that behind him by creating this enormously popular, multi-million-dollar company.

Then, in 1985, everything started to unravel. Amos ran into financial troubles and was forced to sell a majority interest in his company to the billionaire Bass family of Fort Worth, Texas. A few months later, the Bass family sold its share to an investment group. In fact, between 1985 and 1988, Famous Amos went through four changes in management and ownership. Eventually, a Taiwanese food conglomerate acquired it and is still selling Famous Amos–brand cookies. As for its founder, within one year of the initial sale, Amos was just another salaried employee. Frustrated, he left the company in 1989.

But Amos has amazing resilience. Not one to let hardship keep him down, he turned around and started a muffin company that recently was expected to post about $3 million in revenues. Today, he is also a much-sought-after motivational speaker and author of several books. Here are a few of the principles that Amos stuck to throughout his life and that paved his road back to success.

1. *The past is a bucket of ashes.* That's Amos-speak for "Stay focused on the future." When asked about his hard-luck days and previous business problems, Amos intones his "ashes" maxim and steers the topic around to what's ahead. This tendency to look forward got him through the roughest times in his life. When he lost his

multi-million-dollar business and everything around him was falling apart, Amos simply picked himself up and looked around for solutions and new opportunities rather than bemoaning the doors that had closed behind him.

2. *Turn liabilities into assets.* A 1994 court decision added insult to Amos's injury of losing his Famous Amos Cookie Company when it ruled that Wally Amos could no longer call himself Famous Amos or use his name or face to sell cookies. The court reasoned that Amos's name and face were part of the Famous Amos trademark that had been sold off to investors in the mid-1980s. Though the ruling was a devastating blow, denying Amos his key marketing asset, he found a way to capitalize on it. With a sense of irony he launched the Uncle Noname company, a baked-goods business that has been setting the muffin industry on fire.

3. *It's all about teamwork.* Amos lost his Famous Amos Cookies because "I didn't always listen to others," he confesses. "I thought I was invincible. My ego got a little too big for me." Indeed, while his workers were churning out cookies, Amos volunteered to be a spokesman for the Literacy Volunteers of America— a group he remains committed to—and began spending most of his time traveling. Though he was marketing his cookies, he also was busy marketing himself, and at one point he even tried to secure a role for himself in a movie. As his interests wandered, his cookie business began to flounder. Eventually, financial troubles forced him to sell, but the experience taught him an impor-

tant lesson about teamwork. Today, he's singing a different kind of tune—harmony. "I've learned it's all about teamwork. It's not about what I can do, but what we can do together."

4. *Change with changing circumstances.* Amos knew and loved cookies. He knew how to bake them and how to sell them. But the judge's order in 1994 essentially forced him out of the cookie business forever. His solution: muffins. He observed the national trend toward fat-free foods and created a line of tasty fat-free muffins that are selling enormously well. "I'm the muffin man now," he says. "I didn't plan it. Circumstances created it. And you go with what works."

Credits

"Learning from the Giants: Great Motivational Leaders Show How to Find the Inner Flame" was originally published in *Selling Power* as "Motivation: The Inner Flame," by Gerhard Gschwandtner.

"The Zig Is Up" was originally published in *Selling Power* and was written by Malcolm Fleschner.

"New Ways to Win with Dr. Wayne Dyer" was originally published in *Selling Power* as "Wayne Dyer: Space Age Selling Psychology," by Gerhard Gschwandtner, and "New Ways to Win with Wayne Dyer," by James B. Crawford.

Dr. Norman Vincent Peale's "Positive Thinking" was originally published in *Selling Power* and was written by Gerhard Gschwandtner.

"Dr. Denis Waitley: The Seeds of Greatness" was originally published in *Selling Power* as "The Seeds of Greatness," by Gerhard Gschwandtner, and as "National Authority on High-Level Performance, Dr. Denis Waitley, Reveals His Personal Secrets of Success," by Gerhard Gschwandtner.

"Tom Hopkins on Mastering the Art of Motivation" was originally published in *Selling Power* and was written by Gerhard Gschwandtner.

Destined for Success: Motivational Experts and Top Sales Performers Weigh in on What It Takes to Send Your Achievement Levels Soaring" was originally published in *Selling Power* as "Destined for Success: Motivational Experts and Top Sales Performers Weigh in on What It Takes to Send Your Achievement Levels Soaring," by Malcolm Fleschner.

"Stop Waiting for Happiness: 4 Ways to Pursue It" was originally published in *Selling Power* as "Happiness Optional: Instead of Waiting for Happiness to Find You, Try These Four Ways to Pursue It," by Steve Simms.

"Like Yourself Better: 7 Steps for Becoming Your Own Best Friend" was originally published in *Selling Power* as "Seven Ways to Like Yourself Better: To Become Your Own Best Friend, Follow These Seven Steps for a Year," by Steve Simms.

"Inquire Within: When Indecision Stalls Your Quest for Success, Look Inward for Answers" was originally published in *Selling Power* and was written by Jeff Keller.

"Focus on the Positive: 10 Rules for Success" was originally published in *Selling Power* as "10 Rules for Success," by Howard Rackover.

"Let Motivation Work Miracles: 5 Motivational Principles That Will Get You over the Rough Spots" was originally published in *Selling Power* as "Motivation Works Miracles," by Pat Garnett.

"Seek Out Opportunities: Proven Tips for Purpose Driven Sales" was originally published in *Selling Power* as "Motivate Your Sales Team, Purpose Driven Sales," by Geoffrey James.

"Develop a Positive Attitude: 4 Methods for Keeping the Right Mindset" was originally published in *Selling Power* as "Motivate Your Sales Team, Develop a Positive Attitude," by Geoffrey James.

"Sales Manager's Training Guide: 12 Steps to Improve Your

Team's Ability to Cultivate a Positive Attitude That Will Result in Better Sales" was originally published in *Selling Power* and was written by Geoffrey James.

Stories in Part 3, "Motivational Heroes," were originally published in *Selling Power* and were written by Heather Baldwin, Dana Ray, Jacklyn Boice, and Lisa Gschwandtner.

Index

A

ACLU. *See* American Civil Liberties
Union
Adventure of Being a Wife, The (Peale),
45
Adversity. *See also* Fear of failure
antidotes to, 113–115
benefiting from, 81, 90
Denis Waitley on, 68
Mark Monro on, 105–106
Norman Vincent Peale on, 40
overcoming, 11–14, 127–130
Paul Gilanti on, 3–5
Zig Ziglar on, 19
Affirmations:
Norman Vincent Peale on, 10, 57–59
versus positive self-talk, 103–104
role in sales, 10
of self-worth, 118, 125
Ali, Muhammad, 30
American Civil Liberties Union,
180–181
American Girl dolls, 163–164
Amos, Wally, 184–187
Amway, 12
Anderson, Eric, 105
Angela's Ashes (McCourt), 159
Apollo Moon Program, 61–62
Arthur Ashe Award, 175
Ash, Mary K., 6, 110–112
As-if technique, 5–6
Astronauts, 61
Athletes, motivating, 61–62, 64, 66
Attitude. *See also* Negativity; Positive
thinking
Bob Baseman on, 11

Attitude (*Cont.*):
cultivating positive, 149–151
and disappointment, 11
infectiousness of, 115
Norman Vincent Peale on, 41–42
Tom Hopkins on, 90
transforming, 141–147
Wayne Dyer on, 13
Zig Ziglar on, 15–16
Attitude Is Everything (Keller), 141
Audiovisual aids:
motivational, 135, 144
Psychology of Winning, 8
as reinforcement, 18–19, 135
for sales team, 136, 138
Audubon, John James, 166
Audubon, Lucy, 166

B

Bader, Celia, 180, 181
Bannister, Roger, 128
Baseman, Bob, 11
Behavior modification, 62
Belief system. *See* Purposeful living;
Spirituality
Ben & Jerry's, 157
Blockbuster Video, 177
Books:
Dyer's best-selling, 23–26
as learning tools, 18–19, 120
as motivational aids, 57–59, 95, 144
personal library, 136
U.S. reading habits, 64–66
Boston Marathon, 175
Breashears, David, 178
Brennan, Edward A., 173

Brown, Les, 108, 109
Buffett, Warren, 183
Burns, William, 64

C
Career/family, balancing, 114
Carey, Drew, 168
Carnegie, Andrew, 162–163
Carrey, Jim, 168–169
Carrey, Percy, 168–169
Carter, Jimmy, 181
Christian, Kenneth, 98, 100–101
Chrysler Corporation, 167
Chuasiripron, Jenny, 170–171
Churchill, Winston, 126
Claiborne, Frank, 175
Claiborne, Loretta, 175
Clinton, Bill, 181
Cohen, Ben, 157
Columbia University, 179–181
Competition, 26, 30–32
Conant, Lloyd, 74
Confessions of a Grieving Christian
    (Ziglar), 19
Congressional Medal of Honor, 160
Corbett, Mike, 165
Cornell University, 179

D
Daily, Frank, 178–179
Davis, Kevin, 122
Decision-making guidelines, 119–124
Demotivators, 9–14, 85, 91
Detroit Journal, 53
DeVos, Rich, 12–13
Diet, healthful, 17, 136
Dillard University, 169–170
Disney, Walt, 68
Doctors without Borders, 158
Duren v. Missouri, 181
Dyer, Wayne:
    on challenges, 27–32
    influence on Drew Carey, 168
    on mental power, 32–36
    on negativity, 13–14
    persistence of, 110
    philosophy of oneness, 26–27
    on self-worth, 118
    on serenity, 23–27
    on visualization techniques, 36–38

E
Earhardt, Amelia, 161
Eastern philosophy, 31
Ebony magazine, 47
Edison, Thomas A., 68
Edwards, J. Douglas, 85–86
Electrolux, 9
Encyclopedia Britannica, 11
Enlightenment. *See* Self-discovery;
    Spirituality
Exercise. *See* Physical fitness

F
Failure. *See* Fear of failure
Family/career, balancing, 114
Famous Amos Cookies, 184–186
Fathers, influence of:
    on Denis Waitley, 8, 61, 71–72
    on Tom Hopkins, 7–8, 83–84
Fear of failure:
    and decision making, 123–124
    as demotivator, 132–133
    Denis Waitley on, 68–70, 72–74
    Jan Gault on, 96
    Norman Vincent Peale on, 40,
        47–49
    Tom Hopkins on, 84–85, 90–91
    and underachievement, 98
    Wayne Dyer on, 28–29
Ferry, Mike, 107, 109
Field & Stream, 166
Financial success. *See* Money, as meas-
    ure of success
Findlay Carrier, 52
Ford Motor Company, 167
Foreman, Ed, 11–12
Fortune magazine, 163–164
Foundation for Christian Living, The,
    56–57
Freeman, Morgan, 174–175
FreshSuccess, 98, 104
Fripp, Patricia, 109

G
Galanti, Paul E., 3–6
Galyen, Cliff, 99–100
Gault, Jan:
    on affirmations, 103–104
    on defining success, 96, 101
    on goal setting, 102–103

Gault, Jan (*Cont.*):
  on need for action, 106
  on sense of purpose, 100–101
  on underachievement, 98
Getting into Your Customer's Head
  (Davis), 122
Gifts from Eykis (Dyer), 13, 25, 32
Ginsburg, Martin, 179–180
Ginsburg, Ruth Bader, 179–181
Goal setting:
  Denis Waitley on, 63
  Jan Gault on, 97, 102–103
  long- versus short-term, 129
  Michael Jeffreys on, 108–110
  and motivation, 133–134
  Tom Hopkins on, 87
  Zig Ziglar on, 20–22
Goodman, Morris, 127–130
Graham, Don, 184
Graham, Katharine, 181–184
Graham, Phil, 182
Greenfield, Jerry, 157
Grief, dealing with, 19
Grinnell, George, 166
Growth, personal. *See* Self-discovery
Guideposts, 39, 47, 54–55, 56

H
Happiness, choosing, 113–115
Harmony, 26 27
Harris, Joe, 7
Harvard Business Review, 75
Harvard Law Review, 179
Harvard University:
  Ruth Bader Ginsburg at, 179
  Steven McMillan at, 9
Hawaiian Tropic, 108
Health issues. *See* Diet; Physical fitness
Heminger, Lowell, 52
Higher Power. *See* Spirituality
High Exposure (Breashears), 178
Hockenberry, John, 176
Honesty. *See* Integrity
Hopkins, Tom, 6–8
  on demotivators, 84–85, 91
  on failure, 89–90
  as goal setter, 110
  on mentoring, 85–89
  on motivation, 81–84
  as trainer, 79–81, 91–92

Horvath, Kathy, 170
How to Master the Art of Selling
  (Hopkins), 91
Huizenga, H. Wayne, 176–177
Humor, as antidote, 113–114, 158–159

I
Iacocca, lee, 167
Imaging. *See* Visualization
Inferiority, feelings of. *See* Self-doubt
Integrity:
  and self-worth, 117–118
  Tom Hopkins on, 80
International Herald Tribune, 184
Intuition, decision making and, 121
It's a Wonderful Life, 102

J
Jackson State College, 175
Jeffreys, Michael, 107–111
Johnson, John, 47
Johnson, Spencer, 73
Johnson-O'Connor Research Foundation, 71

K
Keller, Helen, 126
Keller, Jeff, 141
Keller, Mike, 172
Kennedy, Danielle, 107

L
Life magazine, 5
Lincoln, Abraham, 68
Literacy Volunteers of America, 157, 186
Lombardi, Vince, 30
Losers, 64–66, 72–74

M
MacArthur, Douglas, 159–160
Madam C.J. Walker Manufacturing, 165
Managers:
  hiring trainers, 122
  motivational tips for, 136–138, 146–147
  relating to objectives of, 134
  role of, 86–88
  training guide for, 149–151

Mandino, Og, 168
Marble Collegiate Church, 39
Mary Kay cosmetics, 6, 111
Mask, The, 169
Mass media, influence of, 144–145,
    150–151
Materialism. *See* Money, as measure of
    success
Mayer, Maria Goeppert, 155–156
McCourt, Frank, 158–159
McMillan, Steven, 9–10
Medecins Sans Frontieres (MSF),
    158
Media. *See* Mass media
Meditation, 121, 123. *See also* Spiritu-
    ality
Meir, Golda, 68
Mentoring:
    Eric Anderson on, 105
    importance of, 7–8
    Tom Hopkins on, 85–88
Meyer, Eugene, 182
Meyer, Katharine, 182
Mighty Power of Your Beliefs, The
    (Gault), 96
Mike Ferry Organization, 109
Miracle Man, The (Goodman), 127
Mission statement, personal, 126
Money, as measure of success:
    Denis Waitley on, 63–64, 75
    versus fulfillment, 95–96, 99–100
    Tom Hopkins on, 81, 92
    Zig Ziglar on, 16–17
Monro, Mark:
    on financial rewards, 99–100
    on positive attitude, 105–106
    on rejection, 104
    on underachievement, 98
Morgan, J.P., 163
Motivation:
    Denis Waitley on, 65
    Mary K. Ash on, 6
    Norman Vincent Peale on, 50
    Paul Galanti on, 3
    principles of, 127–130
    Steven McMillan on, 9–10
    strategies, 131–139
    Tom Hopkins on, 6, 81–82
Mount Everest disaster, 177–178
Music, as motivational aid, 144

N
National Business Hall of Fame, 165
National Public Radio, 176
Navratilova, Martina, 170
Negativity:
    avoiding, 135, 144–146
    as demotivator, 128
    Norman Vincent Peale on, 40,
        43–46
    reversing, 125–126
    and self-worth, 132–133
News media, negativity of, 144–145
Newsweek, 5, 184
New York Times, 183
Nightingale, Earl, 74
Nobel Peace Prize, 158
"No-limit person" theory, 24, 34

O
Obici, Amedeo, 160–161
O'Brien, Dan, 172–173
Ohio Morning Republican, 52
Olympic athletes, 61–62, 64, 69, 173,
    175
One-Minute Manager, The (Johnson),
    73
Optimism, 115, 143. *See also* Positive
    thinking
Ornithological Biography (Audubon),
    166

P
Pak, Se Ri, 170–171
Palmieri, Edmund, 180
Patterson, Grove, 53–54
Pay It Forward, 99–100
Peale, Norman Vincent:
    career path, 39–40
    on failure factors, 47–49
    guidelines for living, 40
    on motivation, 10–11, 50–59
    on positive thinking, 41–47
Peale, Ruth (Mrs. Norman), 45, 56–57
Pentagon Papers, 183
Performance, underachieving, 98
Periu, Omar, 131
Permission to Succeed (St. John), 96
Persistence:
    rewards of, 128–129
    Wayne Dyer's, 110

Personal History (Graham), 182
Peruzzi, Mario, 161
Pessimism. *See* Negativity
Physical fitness:
   Denis Waitley on, 70
   role in decision making, 121
   role in motivation, 135
   Tom Hopkins on, 92
   Wayne Dyer on, 33–34
   Zig Ziglar on, 17
Planters peanuts, 161
Positive thinking. *See also* Attitude
   as action motivator, 128
   versus affirmations, 103–104
   guidelines for, 125–126
   Norman Vincent Peale on, 10–11,
     39–40
   test of, 51
Powell, Colin, 156–157
Power of Positive Thinking, The (Peale),
   39–40, 46, 48
POWs. *See* Prisoners of war
Prayer. *See* Spirituality
Prisoners of war:
   Denis Waitley on, 62, 66
   Paul Galanti as, 3–5
   Wayne Dyer on, 34
Procrastination, 110–111
Products/services, belief in, 133–134
Psychology of Winning, The (Waitley),
   8, 62, 74
Pulling Your Own Strings (Dyer), 13,
   23
Purposeful living:
   and adversity, 114–115
   core beliefs, 100–102, 131–132
   Jan Gault on, 97
   Michael Jeffreys on, 108–109
   role in motivation, 133–134

R
Reagan, Ronald, 42
Reed v. Reed, 180
Reeve, Christopher, 106
Rejection. *See* Fear of failure
Religion. *See* Spirituality
Rice, Ron, 108
Risk-reward relationship, 66, 85, 120
Robbins, Anthony, 107
Rogers, Carl, 13

Rowland, Pleasant T., 163–164
Rutgers University, 180

S
Sadat, Anwar, 68
Sales managers. *See* Managers
Sales meetings, 136–138
Salespeople, successful:
   as action-oriented, 106
   characteristics of, 99–100
   core beliefs and, 100–102
   defining, 95–97
   goal setting, 97, 102–103
   guidelines for, 107–111
   motivating, 136–138, 146–147
   performance issues, 98
   positive thinking, 103–106
   strategies for, 133–136
Sales trainers, needs analysis, 122
Salk, Jonas, 71, 76
San Francisco News, 182
Satori, defined, 31
Sayre, Judson, 58
Sears, Richard, 173
Sears stores, 173
Second Effort, 30
Security, risk versus, 66, 85
Seeds of Greatness, The (Waitley), 62,
   70
Self-discovery:
   role of disappointment in, 13
   Wayne Dyer on, 31–33
Self-doubt:
   Mark Monro on, 98, 105–106
   Norman Vincent Peale on, 48–49,
     52
   Tom Hopkins on, 85
Self-reliance, 114
Self-worth:
   affirmation of, 117–118
   positive versus negative, 131133
   Wayne Dyer on, 27
Selling Power (Rice), 108
Selye, Hans, 71
Simmons, Ruth J., 169–170
Sky's the Limit, The (Dyer), 13, 23, 36
Smith, Gregory White, 171–172
Smith College, 169
SNIOP, defined, 128
Special Olympics, 175

Spirituality:
  in decision making, 123
  Denis Waitley on, 65
  Mary K. Ash on, 6
  Norman Vincent Peale on, 49,
    56–58
  Tom Hopkins on, 92
  Wayne Dyer on, 26–27, 31
  Zig Ziglar on, 19
Sports motivation. *See* Athletes
St. John, Noah, 96
  on affirmations, 103–104
  on goal setting, 103
  on sense of purpose, 101–102
Stanford University, 18–19
Star Search, 168
State Farm, 99
Stoeker, Wendy, 171
*Success Secrets of the Motivational
    Superstars* (Jeffreys), 107
Super Bowl athletes, 61–62

T
Television, negativity of, 144–145
Thomas, Lowell, 55
Thompson, Bob, 161–162
Thompson, Daley, 173
Thoreau, Henry David, 25
'Tis (McCourt), 159
Tolstoy, Leo, 114
Tonight Show:
  Drew Carey on, 168
  Wayne Dyer on, 110
Training:
  motivational meetings, 136–138
  sales manager's guide, 149–151
Transformation, personal. *See* Self-
    discovery
Tutko, Thomas, 64
Twain, Mark, 118

U
Uncle Noname company, 186
University of Florida, 171
University of Idaho, 172
University of Southern California,
    62
University of Success (Mandino),
    168
U.S. Naval Academy, 62

U.S. Supreme Court, 180–181
USS *Hancock,* 3

V
Vietnam War:
  Colin Powell in, 156
  Paul Galanti in, 3–5
  POWs, 62
Visualization:
  Denis Waitley on, 76
  Norman Vincent Peale on, 42–43
  Wayne Dyer on, 36–38

W
Waitley, Denis, 8
  background, 61–62
  on losing, 68–77
  on winning, 62–68
Wake Forest University, 179
Walker, C.J., 164–165
Washington Post, 182–184
Watermelon Magic (Amos), 184
Weathers, Beck, 177–178
Weihenmayer, Erik, 155
Wellman, Mark, 165
*What Do You Really Want for Your
    Children* (Dyer), 14
Whelan, Wendy, 174
Williams, Andy, 76
Winners, characteristics of, 62–64
Winners Edge, The (Waitley), 66, 72
Winning Is Everything (Tutoko and
    Burns), 64
Women in sales, 66

Y
You'll See It When You Believe It
    (Dyer), 36
Your Erroneous Zones (Dyer), 23, 25,
    34, 110, 168

Z
Zaleznik, Abraham, 75
Zen Buddhism, 31
Ziglar, Suzy, 19
Ziglar, Zig:
  background, 15–16
  goal-setting guidelines, 20–22
  on motivation, 7
  recipe for success, 16–19

About the Author

© Hisham Bharoocha

A dual citizen of both Austria and the United States, Gerhard Gschwandtner is the founder and publisher of *Selling Power*, the leading magazine for sales professionals worldwide, with a circulation of 165,000 subscribers in 67 countries.

He began his career in his native Austria in the sales training and marketing departments of a large construction equipment company. In 1972, he moved to the United States to become the company's North American Sales Training Director, later moving into the position of Marketing Manager.

In 1977, he became an independent sales training consultant, and in 1979 created an audio-visual sales training course called "The Languages of Selling." Marketed to sales managers at Fortune 500 companies, the course taught nonverbal communication in sales together with professional selling skills.

In 1981, Gerhard launched *Personal Selling Power*, a tabloid-format newsletter directed to sales managers. Over the years, the tabloid grew in subscriptions, size, and frequency. The name changed to *Selling Power*, and in magazine format became the leader in the professional sales field. Every year

Selling Power publishes the "Selling Power 500," a listing of the largest sales forces in America. The company publishes books, sales training posters, and audio and video products for the professional sales market.

Gerhard has become America's leading expert on selling and sales management. He conducts webinars for such companies as SAP, and *Selling Power* has recently launched a new conference division that sponsors and conducts by-invitation-only leadership conferences directed toward companies with high sales volume and large sales forces.

For more information on *Selling Power* and its products and services, please visit www.sellingpower.com.

Subscribe to *Selling Power* today and close more sales tomorrow!

GET 10 ISSUES – INCLUDING *THE SALES MANAGER'S SOURCE BOOK.*

In every issue of *Selling Power* magazine you'll find:

■ **A Sales Manager's Training Guide** with a one-hour sales training workshop complete with exercises and step-by-step instructions. Get a new guide in every issue! Created by proven industry experts who get $10,000 or more for a keynote speech or a training session.

■ **Best-practices reports** that show you how to win in today's tough market. Valuable tips and techniques for opening more doors and closing more sales.

■ **How-to stories** that help you speed up your sales cycle with innovative technology solutions, so you'll stay on the leading edge and avoid the "bleeding edge."

■ **Tested motivation ideas** so you and your team can remain focused, stay enthusiastic and prevail in the face of adversity.

NEW! Digital Edition same as print. 100% online.

Plus, you can sign up for five online SellingPower.com newsletters absolutely FREE.

FOR FASTEST SERVICE CALL 800-752-7355
TO SUBSCRIBE ONLINE GO TO WWW.SELLINGPOWER.COM

I want a one-year subscription to *Selling Power* magazine.

☐ **YES!** Send me one year of the print edition for only $27

☐ **YES!** Sign me up for one year of the digital edition for only $19

☐ **YES!** Sign me up for one year of both for only $33

Please note: Subscriptions begin upon receipt of payment. For priority service include check or credit card information. Canadian and overseas subscriptions, please visit www.sellingpower.com for rates.

Name: _____ Title: _____

Company: _____

Address:_____

City: _____ State: _____ Zip: _____ Phone: _____

☐ Check enclosed   Charge my ☐ Visa ☐ MC ☐ AMEX ☐ Discover

Card number: _____ Exp.:_____

Name on card: _____ Signature: _____

For fastest service call 800-752-7355 • To subscribe online go to www.sellingpower.com